The Girl With The Iron Jaw
The Amazing Life of Mars Bennett

By John Cosper

In memory of Anton V Foreit, Belle Drummond,
and "Hurricane" JJ Maguire

FOREWORD

What you about to read is a history of one of the women who carved the path in women's wrestling for me. It is an eye opening insight into what the women before me endured. The story of a feisty woman who was destined to become famous in any field she chose, and I am blessed she chose wrestling.

I've said this twice before about two other women wrestlers, Cora Combs and Beverly Shade, and I say it again. "I wish I was 25 years older so I could have been on the road and in the ring with this Lady Wrestler."

The story is of the day to day travels as well as an insight into her personal life. A life cut short in her prime. From a carnival roadie to Air Ballerina to a tough as nails wrestler. She has definitely earned her place in the history of not just women's wrestling but wrestling as a whole. As a famous woman once said, "Put on your seat belts, boys, it's gonna be a bumpy ride."

Looking forward to meeting you in that wrestling arena in the sky, Mars. Thank you for your contribution to our sport.

Vicki Otis
"Princess Victoria"
May 11, 2022

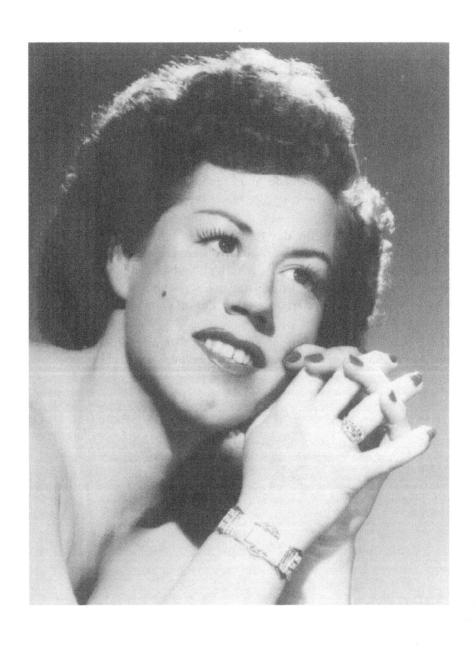

A GIRL NAMED MAUDE

Independent wrestlers have no idea how good they have it today. Sure, they have to work a day job to support their dream. Yes, the promotional hustle is completely on them: maintaining their social media presence, keeping promo photos up to date, relying on fans to share their latest clips, and self-censoring everything so a rash post today doesn't kill their career five years from now.

But let's be honest here. Social media is worldwide. It allowed 4'9" Heather Reckless to get worldwide attention when she was flung from the ring into a crowd of guys during a battle royal. Same goes for Santana Jackson, the Las Vegas Michael Jackson impersonator/professional wrestler who went viral not just for his Moonwalk DDT but his take down of an unruly drunk on Fremont Street.

Heather and Santana didn't have to rely on print media to get their name out. They didn't face the uphill struggle grinding it out in territory after territory, hoping the press not only quotes you accurately but uses the correct photo to promote your latest match.

Such was the case for Mars Bennett when *The Decatur Daily* in Alabama ran a story about her in the May 25, 1952 edition on page twelve. They did a nice job telling the story of how she left the circus behind to become a professional wrestler. But the photo on top of the article? That wasn't Mars. That was June Byers.

No doubt Mars had something to say when she saw the mistake! The fiery, auburn-haired woman with greenish-brown eyes was never shy about speaking up, starting with her name. Show business was family business, after all, going back as far as three generations before Mars.

In the above profile, *The Decatur Daily* mentions that Mars had a great-grandfather and grandmother who performed an aerial act in the circus. Family historians have not been able to put a name to the great-grandfather, but the grandmother in question was a lady named Maude Kyser, who did in fact work in the circus. Maude also became an early star on radio in the 1920s.

Maude's maiden name is unknown, and Kyser is just one of a handful of last names she gained through multiple marriages and divorces. She married to Frank Kyser on September 10, 1898. The couple divorced on August 17, 1905, but before their separation, they became mother and father to a baby girl: Loa "Vivian" Kyser.

Loa Vivian was born on August 20, 1899 in Toledo, Ohio, but not to Maude and Frank. Her birth parents remain a mystery, and the girl was adopted as an infant. Despite the lack of blood relations, it's clear Loa caught the performing bug from her adopted mother Maude.

Maude Kyser owned one of the first radio stations in Detroit or Toledo (again, family records are not certain) and starred on a program called The Lone Wolf. She was an extremely talented performer and a natural fit for radio. She could do twenty-three different kinds of bird calls as well as character voices and sound effects.

Loa Vivian married a man named Anton T. Foreit, a second generation American born in New York on January 21, 1898. Anton T.'s father Paul was one of five children born to Vaclav and Katerina Forejt who had immigrated from Bohemia, Austria in the mid 19th century. He and his wife Anna, who was born in Czechoslovakia, had eight children. Paul and three of his four siblings changed the spelling of their last name to Foreit.

Loa and Anton T. had two children. Their son Anton V. Foreit was born on November 2, 1920. Anton had no middle name, only the initial V to distinguish him from his father. Anton V's little sister was born on August 3, 1922. Loa and Anton T. named her Maude Audrey Foreit.

Anton V. was the first of Loa's children to get a taste of show business when his grandmother Maude cast him in a radio soap opera. She wrote the part specifically for her grandson when he was only about six or seven. Everything on the radio was live in those days, and performing in the show made Anton V. very nervous. Imagine being a young child, a script in your hands, a microphone in your face, knowing that thousands may be listening to you in the comfort of their own homes. It didn't appeal to Anton V. at all, so he asked his grandmother to write him out of the show, which she did.

"My dad often said afterwards that he wished he had stuck with it," says Anton V's daughter Marcella Foreit Robinette. "He said that the people who did radio all seemed to have instant success when they began switching to television, and he wondered if he'd missed out on making some more money."

Anton T. wanted a big family and expected Loa to stay at home and have more children. Loa wanted a career, and their differences led to a divorce. "He wanted eight or nine kids, and she was too much of a party girl for that," says granddaughter Marcella.

The divorce was not a pretty one. Anton T. even went so far as to say the children, Anton V. and Maude Audrey, were not his, even though the kids looked just like him. "They both had a cleft in their chins like Anton T. had," says Marcella Foreit Robinette. "Loa Vivian did not have the same chin. They looked just like their father." Nevertheless, Anton T. wanted nothing to do with them. Eager to become independent and take care of herself, Loa Vivian put the kids in an orphanage so that she could find work.

Anton T.'s parents Paul and Anna were fluent in Czech and did not speak any English. They had a dog named Bum, and they lived near the orphanage where Anton V. and Maude Audrey were sent to live. While out for a walk with his master, Bum recognized the two children playing in the yard outside the orphanage. Paul Foreit did not understand why the dog refused to leave the fence until he looked and saw his grandchildren. Furious, Paul went home and told his son, "Get those kids out of that place and bring them here. No grandchild of mine is going to live in an orphanage!"

Anton V. and Maude Audrey lived with their grandparents for a few years. They were very young, and because they lived with Paul and Anna, their first language ended up being Czech. Years later when Anton V. married a woman from a Polish family, he was surprised to discover he could understand every word she and her family spoke in Polish because the languages were so similar.

Loa Vivian worked for a time as a telephone operator and also got a job at the Hotel Statler, a sixteen story luxury hotel first opened in 1915. Loa might very well have been working at the hotel in October of 1926 when Harry Houdini stayed there while making his final appearance at the nearby Garrick Theater. Once she had established herself career-wise, the kids moved back in with her for a time.

Loa Vivian played as hard as she worked, and she was an alcoholic. Anton V. told his children how his mother would lock him and Mars away in a room while Loa and her friends partied the night away. At a young age, the two kids were shipped off to a farm near Manchester, Michigan to live with the Walkowe family.

The kids worked on the farm in exchange for their room and board. As miserable as that would probably sound to modern kids, Anton V. told his children those were the best years of his life. There were many kids living on the farm, and he fully embraced farm life.

3

Maude Audrey didn't care for it as much. She only lived on the farm a few years before moving back full-time with her mom.

Maude attended Northeastern High School in Detroit, where she became a star athlete. Among other sports, she played basketball and participated in diving and swimming, specializing in the breaststroke. Maude and her brother Anton V. were both athletically gifted, according to Anton V.'s daughter Marcella.

"There are a lot of photos of Mars and my dad doing athletic things on the beach," says Marcella. "She would stand on his shoulders, or he would stand on hers, or she would be doing handstands."

Anton V. told his children that his sister had been good enough in swimming to make the Olympic team, but she was unable to compete. They did not have tampons available in those days, so if a female swimmer was on her period, she was disqualified from competition. Mars unfortunately was unable to compete because of that rule.

Loa Vivian married a Kentucky man named Roy Raymond Skiles. Skiles was a few years younger than Vivian, born in 1903, and he served in the U.S. Armed Forces during World War II.

Roy was a violent man who beat Loa Vivian. One time he beat her bad enough, he broke her nose and some of her ribs. Fifteen year-old Anton V. came home that day and saw what Roy had done to his mother, he attacked Roy and beat him.

Roy called the police. The police took Roy's story and then sat down to speak with Anton V.

"Why did you do this?" they asked.

"Because he broke my mom's nose," said Anton V.

It was then that the police checked out Loa Vivian and saw what Roy had done. The police officer told Roy, "You're lucky you didn't do this to my mom. I would have killed you."

The police didn't do anything to Anton V., who soon decided to run away from home. He enlisted in the Army, lying about his age and claiming that his birth certificate had been destroyed in a fire. He was only fifteen at the time. Anton V. went AWOL from the Army and was later drafted into the Merchant Marines.

Maude Audrey was closer to Loa Vivian than her brother and stayed with her mother. She did, however, make a significant life change as soon as she turned sixteen. While Maude Kyser had given her granddaughter much to be proud of, Maude Audrey Foreit hated her name. She was called Maudie by her family and friends, but even that did not make her happy. Maude and Maudie just didn't sound very "show biz," and the young woman already had her sights on being an entertainer. Right after her sixteenth birthday, she had her first name legally changed to Mars. She went home and told her family never to call her Maudie again.

Mars graduated from Northeastern in 1940. "She was very smart, and she wanted to attend college," says Marcella. "Her mom couldn't afford it, and her dad couldn't pay for it."

Unable to further her education, Mars instead did her part to support the war effort. With so many men overseas, women were needed to take the place of men in the factories. Mars moved west to California and took a job building the U.S. Army Air Force's best hope to defeat the Japanese, the B-29 bomber.

As formidable as the USAAF's B-17 Fighting Fortress proved to be in the skies over Europe, it didn't possess the range needed to fly from friendly air fields in the Pacific to reach the Japanese mainland. The B-29 Superfortress was built specifically to meet that need, a longer range bomber that could make the long haul to Japan and back.

Mars worked on the assembly line of the B-29. In the 1950s news stories would describe her as being the inspiration for Rosie the Riveter. She wasn't, but one look at Mars from a photograph at the time, and it's easy to see why someone would draw that conclusion.

Loa's marriage to Roy Skiles ended during the war when Skiles passed away. He was stateside, still serving in the Army, when he died on February 5, 1943 in Indianapolis. Not long after Roy's death, Loa Vivian made a bold career move: she joined the circus.

Mars left the aircraft business behind around the same time. Many of her co-workers on the line left the factory to get married and become housewives. That was never an option for Mars Foreit. She too chose to run away and join the circus, and if Anton V's version of events is correct, it was Loa who followed her daughter into the business.

Mars always took great pride in talking about her work as a riveter on B-29 aircraft, but Mars never intended to make such work a career. She hadn't changed her name from Maudie to Mars just to have a different name stitched onto her work shirts, and she certainly had no desire for the domesticated life. Mars had the itch to entertain, and that itch led her to join the circus.

In the 1940s the circus was still a huge part of American culture, a yearly event that drew fans by the thousands everywhere they pitched their tents. The circus was the place to see exotic animals: lions, tigers, leopards, bears, elephants, hippos, and rhinos. The circus also presented remarkable human acts like the flying trapeze, the high wire walkers, the acrobats, and the jugglers. And then there were the clowns whose zany antics elicited laughter from children and parents alike.

The circus also included a Midway stocked with all manner of wonders from the human freaks to magicians to wrestling shows. In fact the circus played a significant role in the history of professional wrestling as the sport evolved from a legitimate test of athleticism to a fast-paced brand of entertainment. The circus was also the proving ground for many of Mars Bennett's future colleagues. A handful of professional wrestlers today still speak the Carnie language of the Midway.

There's no record of when or how she first joined the circus, but by 1944, Mars had a foot in the door with the Clyde Beatty-Russell Brothers Circus. Clyde Beatty was the most famous animal trainer of his day, best known for his "fighting style" of working with animals while carrying a whip and a pistol. Throughout his career in the circus, Beatty trained hippos, polar bears, brown bears, lions, tigers, cougars, and hyenas. At the height of his career, he would enter a cage filled with 43 lions and tigers, male and female, a record that still stands.

As mentioned in the previous chapter, Mars did not join the circus alone. Her mother Loa joined up and became a clown, which is how she met the man who would become her life partner, Dippy Diers.

Dippy Diers was a comedian and a circus clown whose credits went beyond the big top. His career began in Vaudeville, where he made a name for himself as a clown and an acrobat. One of his earliest notices came in the September 1912 issue of Variety, where his famous "table act" was first described in print. "Dippy Diers, after some knockabout ground acrobatics, does a "break neck table" trick, featured in the German scene with the acrobatic act of the Six Brachs. Diers fools around with a chair after the manner of Bert Melrose, then casts it aside and standing straight up, starts to sway back and forth on the top of a four table high stand, also like Melrose. After the usual zigzagging, always good for a thrill, Diers goes over with the tables. Not new for New York, but it helps to fill out the variety end of the Hip show."

Diers formed a partnership with fellow Vaudevillian Flo Bennett not long after his debut. Bennett was described as a "capable singer and dancer" and proved to be a perfect match for her partner's pantomime act.

After a quarter of a century of touring the world, Diers joined up with the comedy duo of Ole Olsen and Chic Johnson, appearing on Broadway performing with their shows *Hellzapoppin* in 1938 and *Laffing Room Only* in 1944. When Olsen and Johnson went to Hollywood, they included Diers in their 1943 film *Crazy House*, a madcap comedy that also featured Shemp Howard, Basil Rathbone, Hans Conreid, Allan Jones, Andy Devine, and Count Basie. Olsen and Johnson are best known to more modern film watchers as the namesake of the character Olsen Johnson in Mel Brooks' Western epic *Blazing Saddles*.

Diers also made appearances in the 1942 film *Stars on Parade*, a musical-comedy in the "Hey, kids, let's put on a show!" vein that featured the talents of Nat King Cole, The Chords, and The Ben Carter Choir. His only other credit, at least according to IMDB, was on a 1952 episode of The Buick Circus Hour, a once-a-month fill in on NBC's weekly schedule for the wildly popular Texaco Star Theatre starring another former Vaudevillian, Milton Berle.

Diers and Loa Vivian fell in love. They were never legally married but presented themselves as a married couple where doing so was advantageous, personally or professionally. Loa would carry her second husband's last name Skiles the rest of her life. She was one of the first, if not the first, female clown in the history of the Ringling Brothers Circus. She later went on to work with Elliot Murphy's Aqua Follies in the 1950s.

In the 1944 Program for the Beatty-Russell Brothers Circus, Mars is listed as a Web Girl in an act called Ballet of the Sky. Web girls were acrobats who performed from webs, ropes that had been straightened and then covered with a stitched canvas sheath. Each rope was suspended over the arena and attached to a swivel. A 1944 photo of Mars with her fellow aerialists in the Beatty-Russell Brothers Circus was reprinted in the September 27, 1981 edition of a newsletter called The Circus Report.

Mars and her fellow web girls would ascend the ropes and latch on to a loop near the top. Each girl had a partner on the ground, called a web spinner, who would spin the rope for them. The girls and the web spinners performed carefully choreographed routines to music with the ladies spinning high above the crowd while striking various poses clinging to their webs. The routines were performed without safety nets, making them a thrilling part of every show.

Mars gets a mention in the August 19, 1944 issue of *The Billboard*, an industry publication that covered the business of the circus. The Beatty-Russell Circus played Seattle in early August to large crowds and helped bolster sales of war bonds. The Beatty-Russell crew also took time to celebrate the birthday of "aerial ballet performer" Mars Bennett on August 3.

The Billboard also notes Mars performed as web girl with the Shrine Circus in Houston, Texas in the November 1954 issue. Photos in Mars's scrapbooks show she was still performing aerial acts with the Shrine Circus as late as 1946.

Being a web girl was dangerous but far from being a featured act. The girls who did the webs were considered chorus girls, and it was an introductory act for many circus performers. It was also considered a big deal when a performer no longer had to work the webs. That meant you had really arrived!

One of the first lessons Mars learned in the circus was the importance of picking up as many skills as possible. The more skills you had, the more acts you could join. The more acts you joined, the more you got paid. Mars did everything. She learned how to ride horses and elephants and became part of the animal acts in the show. She became a dancing girl, a clown, an acrobat, and a trapeze artist.

Mars came close to becoming a human cannonball when the man who operated the cannon told her he was looking for a girl to join the act. Mars heard what it paid and said yes. Then the man told her what else he expected of the girl who joined the act. Mars politely told the man where to go; she wasn't doing that!

Mars teamed up with another aerialist named Addie Corsi to form an act known as the Corsimars. They were hailed as part of a fresh crop of stars discovered by John Ringling North on a trek through

Europe, and in 1947, the Corsimars made their debut appearance in the United States with the Ringling Brothers and Barnum & Bailey Circus.

Just a friendly, reminder: the concept of kayfabe became part of pro wrestling thanks to the carnival!

The most daring and dangerous acts the ladies performed was the Iron Jaw, a show-stopping routine in which a man or woman would grip onto a tiny bit with their teeth hooked to the trapeze and fly through the air. The Iron Jaw was hardly a new act. It gained popularity in Europe during the mid-19th century thanks to a woman named Olga Albertina Brown, also known as Miss Lala and Olga Kaire. Lala was a dark-skinned woman of mixed race who also mastered the trapeze and the high wire, among other skills. Not only could she hang and spin by her teeth from the Iron Jaw, she could also support other acrobats with her teeth. She would hook two (or sometimes just one) knee through the trapeze, hanging upside down while gripping a bit in her teeth that supported another acrobat. As if that weren't amazing enough, Lala could also support two more trapeze artists with her arms while holding one up with her teeth. For a grand finale, Lala would lift an iron canon with her teeth that would be fired even as she hung upside down.

A 1947 photo shows Mars hanging upside down, her strong legs wrapped around a trapeze bar, holding a strap with both hands. Addie is on the other end of the strap, gripping the strap with her teeth with another strap wrapped around her head. One such photo, still in possession of Mars's family, has an inscription written to her mother:

Mommie —
I Iere's your baby really earning her money.
Love always —
Mars

You have to wonder if Loa didn't join the circus to keep a closer eye on her baby while she earned that money!

There are no photos showing Mars and Addie in the reverse position. Nor are there any photos showing Mars performing the Iron Jaw herself with any other partners. Nevertheless, Mars would take one of her most famous nicknames in the wrestling business from this act, becoming The Girl With The Iron Jaw. Regardless whether she "earned" the moniker in the circus, she most definitely earned it from wrestling.

Mars spent at least two years working for The Ringling Brothers and Barnum & Bailey Circus, the most famous of all the American circuses. The company's history goes back to the 1860s when James Bailey and partner James E. Cooper formed one of the country's first traveling shows. P.T. Barnum, a legendary showman, producer, and museum curator, lent his name to a new traveling circus founded in 1871. Barnum and Bailey competed with one another for a decade before merging their shows in 1881.

The Ringling Brothers of Baraboo, Wisconsin founded their own circus in 1884, but it wasn't until 1905, when surviving partner James Bailey sold the Barnum & Bailey show to the Ringlings, that The Greatest Show on Earth finally merged into one.

Mars does not appear in any of the Ringling Brothers and Barnum & Bailey Circus programs by name, but The Corsimars are listed in the 1947 program as part of Display 2, described as featuring "Unparalleled and desperately hazardous midair sensations. Fellow aerialists featured in Display 2 include Jimmy Millette, The Merions, Albert Powell, The Rose Sisters, Ira Millette, and Natal 'Monkey or Man?'"

The Milliner Library at Illinois State University, keepers of the Passion for Circus media collection, have two color photos of Mars from 1947. In one, Mars can be seen solo wearing a pink, feathered head piece, a pink ruffled dress, and black stockings, visible as Mars lifts her skirt high to show off her legs. In the other, Mars is dressed in a purple men's madrigal outfit while standing beside Bella Attardi, who is dressed in a matching purple madrigal gown. It's clear from the photos Mars put her talents to use any place she could, not just on the flying trapeze.

Mars returned to The Greatest Show on Earth in 1948. Again, she's not mentioned by name, but she's listed in the Route Book for 1948, and her name pops up several times throughout the year in conjunction with the circus, beginning with a photo in *The Boston Globe*. Photos in her scrapbook show she was part of the Monte Carlo Aerial Ballet.

In the April 18, 1948 edition of *The Boston Globe*, Mars can be seen doing a handstand in the background while a couple of prop men work on a piece of the circus set in Madison Square Garden. The attached article by K.S. Barlett captures the atmosphere around Mars as the Greatest Show on Earth prepared to open in New York.

The train from Sarasota, Florida arrived on Friday afternoon, April 9, but the crew of workmen, musicians, acrobats, animals, and other performers had to sit back and wait patiently. Hockey was still in session at the Gardens, and as much as everyone wanted to get on with the show, they would have to wait until the Rangers played their final game of the year.

On Sunday night, April 11 at 10:15 p.m., the last of the New York Rangers skated off the ice. Fans exiting the Arena can't help notice a maze of "strange apparatus under the rafters." Work crews moved in as soon as the crowd had departed. They were now less than three full days away from opening night, and not since 1937 had the circus been given such a short window of time to prepare for their season opener.

Twelve hours later, 10:15 a.m. on Monday morning, all the ice is now gone, replaced by dirt that continues to be brought in by truck. Stages are being erected. Sections of the performance rings are put in place. Painters, carpenters, and tradesmen of all sorts work on everything from dressing rooms to animal quarters. John Ringling North, producer and president of the company, and his brother Henry Ringling North, John's assistant and vice president, were both keeping an eye on the proceedings.

By 3:30 p.m. Monday afternoon, the last shovel of dirt falls into place as a whistle blows and the first rehearsals begin. Rehearsals will occupy the rest of the day and all of Tuesday. The elephants are put through their paces. The high wire and trapeze troupes check and double check their apparatus has been installed with the utmost care. The lighting crew runs through their cues. A costume mistress frantically modifies a frilly dress for Susie the chump after one of the producers deems it to be too short. Merle Evans, director of the circus band, has his merry musicians in place to accompany each act, many of them putting in their first ever performance at the Gardens.

At 8:30 p.m. Tuesday everyone is in place as the first full dress rehearsal begins. At 4:30 p.m. the following day, an equestrian act trots across the dirt floor to the exit, marking the end of rehearsals. Four hours later, The Ringing Brothers and Barnum & Bailey Circus kicked off its inaugural performance of the 1948 season.

Mars is never listed by name in the Ringling Brothers programs of the time, but she's mentioned twice in *The Billboard* during 1948. In addition to marking her birthday in August, the June 1948 issue noted that Mars played in a baseball game between the girls and the midgets. Originally scheduled for Washington D.C., the game had to be postponed due to rain until the circus reached Philadelphia. Mars hit the first home run of the game, but the midgets, looking dapper in their brand new uniforms, beat the ladies 10 to 5.

When Mars left the circus behind, she took a special companion with her. Blondie was a three year old fox terrier described as being "luggage tan" with a white face, white paws, and a white tail. Like Mars, she had performed with the Clyde Beatty Circus and the Ringling Brothers show. Mars took Blondie with her when she went into the wrestling business, and in 1952, she would make headlines of her own.

Mars took much more than a furry friend with her when she switched careers. Many of the skills Mars developed in the circus translated to professional wrestling. She was known for tumbling and acrobatics in the ring, and her willingness to take risks and endure a little pain certainly made her a fearless performer. Even clowning had its benefits, as WWE star Becky Lynch attested when she spoke to Wrestling Inc's William Windsor about why she attended clown college.

"It's actually [a] really powerful acting technique because you put on this little red nose and it's like an arrow to your eyes and they say that the eyes are the windows to the soul. It's like people can see through you or you feel like that. There's just this thing that comes over you when you have that little red nose on you."

It's not hard to see how donning some makeup and learning to play the fool might make you a better pro wrestler.

Left: Loa Vivian and Anton T. Foreit. Right: Mar's grandmother Maude Foley and her boyfriend Chief Redpath. (Courtesy Marcella Foreit Robinette.)

Anna and Paul Forejt with their grandchildren Maude Audrey and
Anton V. (Courtesy Marcella Foreit Robinette.)

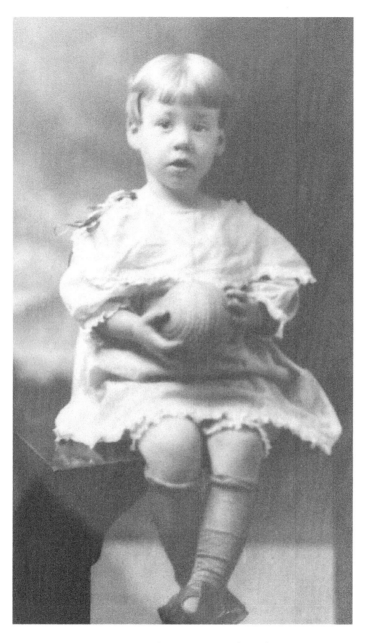

Maude Audrey Foreit, before she learned to hate her name. (Courtesy Marcella Foreit Robinette.)

Anton V, Maude (Mars), and Loa Vivian Foreit. (Courtesy Marcella Foreit Robinette.)

Top: Mars and Anton V as kids and all grown up on the beach. Bottom: Mars (third from left in the front row) and her high school swim team in 1939. (Courtesy Marcella Foreit Robinette.)

Maude (soon to be Mars) as a teenager. (Courtesy Marcella Foreit Robinette.)

Clockwise from top left: Clyde Beatty and Mars; Mars and Loa Vivian; Mars and a lion cub; Loa Vivian and Dippy Diers. (Courtesy Marcella Foreit Robinette.)

Top: Monte Carlo Aerial Ballet 1948. Minnie Alan, Mars, Rusti Kurka, Joan Sharkey, Frannie McCoskey, Irene Ubel. Bottom: Jean Skeeter, Concha Escalante, Mitz Skeeter, Kay Burslem, Mars, Melouga Escalante, Butch Krause, Betty Escalante.

Mars performing on the webs. (Courtesy Marcella Foreit Robinette.)

Laura May Petrillo and Mars pose with former circus performer Burt
Lancaster at a December 1948 celebrity circus.

In sync with aerial partner Addie Corsi. (Courtesy Marcella Foreit Robinette.)

Mars and Addie Corsi perform the Iron Jaw. (Courtesy Marcella Foreit Robinette.)

PIN UP GIRL

During her down time in her circus days, Mars worked out at Bothner's Gymnasium, a private workout facility located right above the 42nd Street Automat in New York City. Founder George Bothner was once a top claimant to the World Lightweight Wrestling Championship and a long-time friend of the legendary George Hackenschmidt. He competed in his first amateur tournament in 1884 and soon joined the New York Athletic Club. Bothner turned pro and became the World Lightweight Champion in 1903 after defeating the English Champion Tom Riley. He lost the title three years later to Eugene Tremblay.

In 1914 he took the money he'd saved from his year of wrestling and opened the gym that bore his name. He continued to wrestle professionally until the age of 53, but his focus shifted to training. He even took part in a Jiu Jitsu exhibition at the White House given for President Theodore Roosevelt.

Bothner was in his early 80s in 1948. His wrestling days were behind him, and he had only recently given up working out with trainees at the gym. He was a bit senile at the time Mars would have crossed paths with him, but he had a soft spot for the ladies who trained in the gym. He would often serve them cherry pie and hot coffee in the middle of their workouts.

Mars trained with Lou Leonard, the gym supervisor who was also purported to be the foremost expert on judo and jiu-jitsu in the United States at that time. In a 1947 Street and Smith sports comic, a 110-pound woman was depicted throwing her instructor using the techniques of jiu jitsu as taught by Leonard. It's not hard to see the appeal of such arts to a woman like Mars, who lived for physical activity. Mars trained in weightlifting, judo, boxing, and wrestling. Her interest in the fight sports led to a few appearances in the "cheesecake" magazines of the day.

Hardly a new phenomenon by the late 1940s, these pin-up magazines catered to a largely male audience by publishing photos of women in sexy attire or provocative poses. The magazines helped to launch the careers of future stars like Marilyn Monroe, Yvonne DeCarlo, Veronica Lake, Sophia Loren, Brigitte Bardot, and Jayne Mansfield.

Women's professional wrestling had everything the pin-up publishers wanted: physically fit women in skin-tight attire entangling their bodies on the mat. Eagle-eyed photographers would snap hundreds of photos and choose the most sensational to feature in the large, black and white pages of their publications.

Beauty Parade featured Mars and a woman named Ruth Murney in a two-page photo spread for their August, 1948 issue. Under the heading of "Swing It, Baby," readers discovered Mars Bennett grinning ear to ear as she held Miss Murney over her shoulders in a fireman's carry. Another photo below shows Mars on top of Ruth, forcing her into a pin position.

On the opposite page, the girls are seen not only wrestling but boxing. In almost every photo, Mars has the upper hand.

In May of 1949 the publication *Picture Show* ran a two-page spread featuring a group of lady wrestlers managed by former wrestler Billy Wolfe: Elvira Snodgrass, Nell Stewart, Ann Laverne, Mae Weston, and Violet Viann. Just one page away, the magazine also published a photo of Mars Bennett, an overhead shot in which she held a well-built, shirtless man over her shoulders in an airplane spin. Mars wasn't featured with the lady wrestlers but included in another photo essay depicting women doing things traditionally associated with men. "Mars Bennett, strong lady who has perfected herself in judo, weightlifting, wrestling, and boxing, may not be typical, but she is proof that a woman is not traditionally the weaker sex."

A month later, *Hit!* magazine released an issue with the headline "Girl Acrobat Wrestles" on the front cover. Mars is once again the subject, shown in a series of photos that showcase her acrobatic skills as well as her growing interest in fight sports.

"A strikingly pretty brunette, she tips the scales at 125, is amazingly proportioned, graceful, and smooth muscled. Performing on the high-flying rings has given her the shoulder and back development of a middleweight boxer. In New York, where the circus tenants Madison Square Garden, Mars spends her time in George Bothner's famous gym. [A] light workout for her includes high-bar, rings, abdominal board, and twenty minutes with barbells, after which she's sufficiently loosened up to indulge in thirty minutes of wrestling."

Mars is pictured on the rings and the high-bar as well as working barbells with her legs. She's also shown grappling with a woman named Marie Gallagher while Lou Leonard, a former Navy judo instructor, plays referee. A *Hit!* reader from New York City, where women's wrestling was illegal, loved the photos of Mars and Marie Gallagher so much, he wrote a letter to the magazine that was later published.

Dear Editor:

As one of the disgruntled New Yorkers who has been deprived of his favorite sport, "watching the gals wrestle," by local authorities, I can't get enough pictures of the girls in action. The trouble is that many of the photos which appear in magazines and newspapers are too staged. Recently, you had a feature on Marie Gallagher and Mars Bennett, a couple of femmes who really mix it up. May I see more of this pair?

B.H.

Not only did *Hit!* publish more photos of Mars and Marie, the ladies also appeared in *The Police Gazette*, one of the oldest men's periodicals in America that specialized in sports reporting and photos of lovely ladies. The *Gazette* also did a single-page spread featuring Mars and her circus partner Addie Corsi showcasing their strength and flexibility as well as performing the Iron Jaw.

It's hard to know how many times Mars appeared in cheesecake publications, but it's clear she was a popular attraction, especially for men who liked a woman with muscles. Under headings like "Queens: Curves or Biceps?" "Beauty on the Mat," "Belle of the Barbells," and "Who's The Weaker Sex?" magazines printed photos of Mars and sometimes Marie Gallagher not only battling each other but twisting Lou Leonard in knots.

While many of the photos shoots focused on the thrill of watching a woman and a man or two women grapple with one another, others showcased Mars and her incredible muscle power. Mars can be seen balancing a one hundred pound barbell over her shoulders, lifting a seventy-five pound barbell over her head with one hand, and lying on her back while balancing a 150 pound barbell on the bottoms of her feet.

Lou Leonard took the place of iron weights in a few photos that truly revealed Mars's power. One photo shows Mars lying on her back holding a 100-pound barbell over her head while she holds Lou Leonard in the air by her feet. In another, Mars is also on her back, her hands straight up in the air, balancing Lou Leonard and his full weight as his hands and knees are on Mars's open palms. Another shows Mars in the air, holding onto a pair of gymnast rings, while she holds Lou Leonard in the air, locked between her powerful legs.

"Note the apparent ease and lack of strain with which she handles both barbells and instructor Leonard, and you'll understand why she is called the foremost all-around girl athlete of our times."

Mars truly loved New York City. She loved the night life, and she loved the theater and meeting the big stars. She became friends with at least two Broadway actresses, Mary Healy and Mary Beth Hughes, both of whom went on to Hollywood and starred in B-movies. Mars kept photographs she'd taken with both ladies that had been signed by Healy and Hughes. Mars amassed quite a collection of autographs over the years, but most of those photos and signatures vanished after she passed away.

In her wrestling days, it was frequently mentioned that Mars herself had traveled to Hollywood and performed stunt work on a few movies. One newspaper account in Chester, Pennsylvania from 1950 even said Mars had minor roles in three films: *The Snake Pit*, a 1948 drama starring Olivia de Havilland; *Pinky*, Elia Kazan's controversial 1949 drama about race; and Cecil B. DeMille's *Samson and Delilah*, a 1949 biblical epic that also featured Wee Willie Davis in a small role.

Another source indicates that Mars did stunt work in *Trapeze*, a 1956 film starring Burt Lancaster. Mars would have been a natural fit for the circus film given her resume, and she did cross paths with Lancaster at a celebrity circus event in 1948.

Not surprisingly, IMDB does not list Mars as working on these films or any other. Movies did give stunt performers their due credit during that time, so if she did work in the pictures, it was as an uncredited extra, stunt person, or both. The Chester newspaper's claim is interesting but dubious. The same article has Mars lettering eleven times in sports while attending an Oklahoma teacher's college and playing professional softball with the Kansas City Redheads, where she "created quite a stir as the leading catcher." Both claims are false.

MARS MEETS MILLIE

Despite all her successes in the circus, Mars always had people trying to persuade her to try a different line of work. "Yeah, people used to stop me and suggest I turn to wrestling, even when I was happy with the circus," she said in 1950. "It got to be a regular line with some fellows. Like they say to some girls, 'You oughta be in pictures.'" Given she had developed a taste for the fight sports during her time at Bothner's Gym, it was inevitable that the world of pro wrestling would come calling.

It's very possible that Billy Wolfe himself spotted her in the pages of a magazine and set out to recruit her. Wolfe was also a regular visitor to Bothner's Gymnasium, and more than a few ladies worked out at the gym in the hopes of meeting the women's wrestling mogul. Mars had her own legend she liked to spin, a story involving the greatest women's champion of all time, Mildred Burke.

Mildred Burke had once been a dreamer herself. A child bride at the age of seventeen, Millie Bliss fell in love with professional wrestling when her first husband Joe Shaffer took her to see the matches. Her husband laughed when she told him that she wanted to take up pro wrestling. Women had been wrestling professionally nearly as long as men, but the prevailing view in the early 1930s held that women were too delicate for such a physical undertaking.

One man who saw the potential for women's wrestling as a money-making endeavor was former light heavyweight wrestler Billy Wolfe. Wolfe was nearly twice Millie's age when the two met at the Kansas diner Bliss ran with her mother. After several weeks of serving Wolfe and his then-love interest Barbara Ware, Bliss told Wolfe she wanted to become a pro wrestler. Wolfe scoffed at the idea. Millie was small and petite, especially compared with Ware. She was also pregnant with her only son Joe.

After Joe's birth, Millie renewed her push to make Billy Wolfe train her. She was divorced with an infant son, and the bills were mounting. Wolfe finally relented and gave her a tryout. Long story short: Wolfe saw potential in the tiny waitress. Millie Bliss became Mildred Burke, and Wolfe became her trainer, business partner, and husband.

Their marriage was more about business than matrimonial bliss. Wolfe was a chronic womanizer who slept with most of the ladies he employed. Burke would have an affair with G. Bill Wolfe, Billy's son. But as business partners, Billy Wolfe and Mildred Burke took women's wrestling from side show carnivals of the mid-1930s to the main event scene in the arenas a decade later.

Mars would often draw comparisons to Mildred Burke because of her stature, her looks, and her physique. Mildred Burke was pin up fave herself for the same reason Mars was. Both of the ladies appealed to the men who liked girls with big muscles.

It's unclear when Mars decided to make the leap from the circus ring to the wrestling ring, but the legend Mars told involved a chance encounter at the Ringling Brothers's winter quarters.

"It was in Sarasota, Florida... that I met Mildred Burke, the famous lady wrestling champion. She was a visitor on the lots and later I saw her perform. I guess my talk with her inspired me to finally go into wrestling. I never forgot my talk with her because after I took a nasty fall, I retired from circus work, contacted her, and, well, here I am in professional wrestling."

A more dramatic version of the Mildred and Mars story has Mars falling thirty-five feet from the trapeze the same day, just a few hours after the two women met. Her conversation with Burke fresh on her mind, Mars decided then and there she was ready to leave the circus behind.

Mars also credited the legendary boxing champ Jack Dempsey for encouraging her to pursue wrestling. Mars was in Hollywood still recovering from her fall when she stopped by Dempsey's house to take a dip in his pool. "He had watched my act on the trapeze, and he also knew I was on friendly terms with Mildred Burke. 'Mars,' he said, 'Why don't you take Mildred's advice. Get into lady wrestling. I know you'll do well.' I got to listening to Jack and finally he swayed me."

Whether Mildred Burke or Jack Dempsey had anything to do with Mars's career change may never be known, but her family is certain Mars had more than one reason for making the switch. She was thinking about the future. Mars had a dream to open a high end restaurant in New York City. That dream required money, and Mars could make more money faster as a wrestler than a trapeze artist.

Mars moved to Columbus, Ohio, home base for Mildred Burke and Billy Wolfe's girl wrestling empire, to begin her training. Belle Starr, who broke in four years after Mars, described what training was like for a newbie in a 2007 interview with Slam! Wrestling's Jamie Hemmings.

"They put us in the ring. You were trained by all the different lady wrestlers like Mae Weston, June Byers, Mildred Burke," said Starr. "They had medicine balls and they would throw them at you. They would just throw you all over the ring. If you weren't able to keep up with it, you'd either hurt your back or leg or something. I was very thin, I was not very heavy. I used to hear, 'Oh she'll never make it.' But then they'd say, 'We keep throwing everything at her and she keeps coming back!'"

As fit as Mars was from her circus and gym training, she was made to keep coming back. "I had a tough time the first few months," Mars admitted to *Wrestling and Boxing* writer Charles A. Smith in 1952. "Naturally, Billy Wolfe did all he could to make it easy for me. I picked up wrestling quickly. It came to me naturally, and the acrobatic work and the tumbling helped a lot too. But I took some beatings until I learned to dish it out as well as take it. It took a few bouts to make me realize that I wasn't just in the ring to give a wrestling exhibition. I was in there to win."

When a girl was ready to start performing in front of crowds, Billy Wolfe sent her to wrestle in the carnivals, just as he had with Mildred Burke. The girls would hone their skills in the "At Shows" on the circus Midway until he deemed them ready to work the wrestling shows in the arenas.

Mars took plenty of lumps in those circus matches, but she persevered. She gave a great deal of credit to Mildred Burke for encouraging her along the way. Burke gave Mars hope that she would succeed, that she would become a main event star, and that one day, she would snatch the title belt secured around Mildred Burke's waist for herself.

STEPPING INTO A NEW RING

By the spring of 1950, Mars was ready for her debut on a professional wrestling show. The earliest ad for a Mars Bennett match appeared in *The North Adams Transcript* on April 3, 1950. The show took place at the North Adams State Armory in Massachusetts on April 6, and despite Mars's rookie status, the lady wrestlers were the primary attraction.

Mars stood at 5'3" and weighed 140 pounds. Newspapers often described her build as husky or powerful, always accentuating her muscular physique. She would have compared favorably to modern day star Jordynne Grace: short of stature, but fit and muscular. Beautiful, but physically not someone you want to trifle with!

Billy Wolfe liked his girls to look and dress like ladies outside the ring, and Mars certainly fit the bill. She was a gorgeous woman with a winning smile who knew how to strike a pose for the cameras. She was always well-dressed in public, always tanned thanks to endless hours sunbathing, and always in tip-top physical condition.

Glamour girl Mars was billed from Hollywood. Her opponent that night was Carolyn Copeland of Cincinnati, according to the ad, and the ladies were to wrestle to one fall with no time limit. Three other matches were advertised with no names listed. Admission was a dollar for general admission or $1.50 for ringside.

A few promotional photos of Carolyn Copeland survive, but details about who she was are sketchy. Newspapers in the South from August of 1950 describe her as an auburn-haired beauty from Florida and a former Miss Miami in the 1948 Atlantic City Miss America contest.

At the end of April, Mars was in the Midwest, wrestling in Evansville, Indiana, and billed as a native of Nebraska. From Evansville she went to Louisville, Kentucky, where she wrestled at the Columbia Gym on Fourth Street for the Allen Athletic Club in a match against June Byers.

Standing at 5'7" and billed at 150 pounds, June Byers was a six-year veteran at the time Mars broke in. She was born DeAlva Eyvonnie Sibley on May 25, 1922, and her uncle Ottaway Roberts worked for promoter Morris Siegel in Byers's hometown of Houston, Texas. Byers would get in the ring and learn what she could from Siegel's crew after the shows, which is how she caught the eye of Billy Wolfe. Byers jumped at the chance to join Wolfe's crew when the offer was extended. She was divorced and nearly broke when she became a lady wrestler, and she slowly began to rise up the ranks.

June was not only one of the taller ladies in professional wrestling but one of the hardest hitters. She especially loved delivering a chop right across the chest, knocking the wind out of her opponent. The other ladies hated it, but they learned that the best way to work with June was to give back as hard as you got. If June sensed any weakness, she would rip you apart. For Mars, it would have been trial by fire every night working with the tall Texan.

June was no stranger to the wrestling scene or to Louisville. Many fans remembered the night in January of 1947 when she defeated Dot Dotson at the Jefferson County Armory (which later became the Louisville Gardens) before coming back out to be maid of honor for a wrestling wedding. The bride was Miss Perma Crook, and her groom, Gil Woodworth, had earlier entertained the crowd by wrestling a seven-foot long American alligator.

Mars and June battled to a draw that night, going to the fifteen minute time limit plus another five minutes with no decision. Matchmaker Francis McDonogh announced that the ladies would appear again on Friday's Derby Eve show, the night before the Kentucky Derby.

Mars and June squared off the following night in Evansville, where Mars defeated June two falls out of three to earn a title shot against Mildred Burke. Two nights later, Mars defeated June in Louisville, two falls out of three, but in an ironic twist, June Byers once again found herself upstaged by an animal on the undercard. As exciting as the ladies bout was, the fans left talking about how Pete Peterson and Floyd Bird came out on the losing end in a handicap match versus Ginger the Wrestling Bear.

Mars and June were sent West the following week with Lily Bitter and Millie Stafford. Lily and Millie were both fairly new to the business just like Mars. Millie Stafford's first recorded match took place in 1949. She was noted to be a skilled swimmer, ice skater, and basketball player prior to becoming a lady wrestler. A native of Minneapolis, the 5'3", 138 pound Stafford was trained by Racine, Wisconsin promoter Einar Olsen before leaving her job as a telephone operator for the grappling game.

Lily Bitter, who debuted in 1950, was a former five-and-dime store clerk from Newark, New Jersey, who found wrestling to be a more exciting and lucrative career. The short-haired brunette was listed at 140 pounds and distinguished herself from the pack by wrestling barefoot.

The four ladies wrestled in Arizona, Colorado, and Wyoming, switching dance partners as they worked singles matches against one another. Mars came out on top in all her matches, a sign great things were expected from her, and several of her victories were touted as earning her a title shot against Mildred Burke.

Oddly enough, Mars and June once again found themselves sharing the spotlight with an animal in Phoenix. On Monday night May 15, the third match on the card pitted Terry McGinnis and Bob Kennison against Mel Peters and Farmer Burns, the Arkansas hillbilly who never went anywhere without his pet pig!

Three of the ladies may have been rookies, but all indications are the fans got a show no matter who was in the ring. The *Casper Star-Tribune* published a photo of Mars Bennett on top of Millie Stafford with a pair of men's legs and feet sticking out the bottom of the pile. The legs belonged to referee Curley LaFleur, who had his shirt ripped twice that evening: once by King Kong Cox, and once by Millie Stafford.

Mars developed a style in the ring that showcased her strength, speed, and athleticism. She was known for her flying mares, back breakers, and airplane spins, and she impressed fans with her ability to take some hard knocks from opponents. Mars also threw in plenty of cartwheels and other acrobatic flourishes in homage to her circus roots.

Mars took on the babyface role in these early matches, taking the brunt of the hair-pulling and dirty deeds from Millie, Lily, and June, but the reporter for the *Star-Tribune* indicated that despite appearances, Mars was no angel herself. "The air around the ring hung heavy with the smell of makeup and perfume. Neither girl looked like a candidate for sportsmanship honors as they pulled hair and performed other unniceties."

In June Mars went to the Carolinas to work for promoter Jim Crockett against Beverly Lehmer. Originally from Council Bluffs, Iowa, Beverly and her sister Carolyn sold concessions and tickets for the local promoter. When Carolyn expressed interest in the business, Beverly was coerced into being her training partner. Just seventeen years old, she was photographed holding George Temple, brother of Shirley Temple, in an airplane spin hold for the newspapers.

Billy Wolfe offered Beverly $100 a week to work for him - double what her father was making working on the railroad. Of course Billy Wolfe would end up taking half her earnings, but she stuck it out two and a half years before stepping away from the business for a time.

It's always amusing to see how the local promoters present new wrestlers. Crockett listed Mars as being from Louisville, Kentucky, and Lehmer from Columbus, Ohio. Both are wrong, and as we've already seen, Mars has had several hometowns other than Detroit listed in the papers. In the coming months she would also be billed as a native New Yorker and a ranch gal from Oklahoma. This was 1950, and since no one in the Carolinas saw the papers from Arizona, it didn't matter if the stories didn't match up.

Case in point, the Jack Dempsey connection put out by Jim Crockett in the build up to this match. The Richmond, Virginia, and Charlotte newspapers ran stories about how Jack Dempsey had encouraged Mars to go into professional wrestling, as Mars always claimed. However, the South Carolina newspaper said that Beverly Lehmer, not Mars, was a protege Dempsey.

The fans in the Carolina towns were none the wiser. Both versions of the story sold tickets, and the ladies did not disappoint. The girls were a hit from Columbia to Richmond to Greensboro to Charlotte. Jim Crockett himself declared their clash in Charlotte to be one of the best he had ever seen. Then again, Jim Crockett said Beverly Lehmer - or was it Mars Bennett? - was discovered by Jack Dempsey!

Mars reconnected with June Byers, Millie Stafford, and Lily Bitter for a tour of the Midwest, working cities like Anderson, Greenfield, and Richmond in Indiana as well as Dayton, Cincinnati, Chillicothe, Canton, Newark, and Mansfield in Ohio. The girls would often split up to work singles matches on different cards, but at other times they'd pair up for tag bouts, such as the June 16 match in which Mars and June defeated Lily and Millie. They were joined on the road later in the month by Beverly Lehmer, Jean Holland, and Marylin Martin. On July 1, all seven women capped off their Midwestern run with a battle royal broadcast live on WLWT television in Cincinnati.

In July Mars headed East with June, Millie, and Lily to work New Jersey, Maryland, and DC. Mars and Millie worked the main event in Asbury Park, New Jersey under the watchful eye of guest referee Max Baer, the former heavyweight boxing champion of the world.

Mars earned high praise in Vineland, New Jersey following a match with Lily Bitters. *The Daily Journal* declared both women to be superior grapplers to the men working the June 13 card while comparing Mars to the legendary champion Jim Londos.

The ladies put on another televised battle royal on July 28 in Akron, Ohio before moving South in late July to wrestle in Tennessee and Louisiana. Their run in Louisiana culminated with a couple of five-woman battle royals that also included veteran Dot Dotson and a new girl from Hazard, Kentucky, Cora Combs.

Jim Crockett welcomed Mars back in August for a second run. Lily Bitter took Millie Stafford's place for a series of singles matches against Mars after Millie was injured in Houston. The barefooted Lily seemed to relish playing the heel to Mars's hero, giving referee "Cyclone" Copley a beating in Columbia, South Carolina before taking a cartwheel-powered kick to the chin from Mars that cost her the match.

Lily and Mars continued their rivalry in a series of tag matches. They worked the Carolina-Virginia circuit a second time with Beverly Lehmer in Mars's corner and Carol Cook joining Lily.

It was when Mars returned to the Midwest that the newspapers began calling her The Girl with the Iron Jaw. Mars may not have been the girl holding the leather bit in her mouth, but wrestling fans had come to appreciate her tenacity when taking a punch in the jaw.

Mars found herself working with a new crop of ladies in the fall. She wrestled Ada Ash, the wife of Al Szasz who was known for grappling alligators as well as women. She faced Ellen Olsen and Eva Lee, two newer members of Billy Wolfe's group, as well as ten year veteran Ann Laverne. But when she got to Texas in September, she spent most of her time battling one of the toughest women in the history of pro wrestling: Johnnie Mae Young.

Born in Sand Springs, Oklahoma on March 12, 1923, Mae Young joined up with Billy Wolfe and company when she was just a teenager. Mae was part of a core group that built women's wrestling into a main event attraction during the 1940s, mixing it up with the likes of Elvira Snodgrass, Mae Weston, Gladys "Kill 'Em" Gillam, and of course the women's champion Mildred Burke. She was one of the first women to wrestle in Canada, and she enjoyed a second career in wrestling started in 1999 when the WWF began booking her for appearances alongside The Fabulous Moolah.

There are countless stories and legends about Mae Young stretching back to her wrestling days. She left the business for a time to become a traveling evangelist. She also may have driven a man out to the desert and left him for dead. While many of the ladies enjoyed dressing and making themselves up like ladies, Mae loved to wear pants, drink beer, smoke cigars, play cards, and get into fist fights when cards got out of hand.

The September 22, 1950 show at the Sam Houston Coliseum in Houston drew 6,500 fans. Promoted as the 35th anniversary of shows under the direction of promoter Morris Siegel, every seat was just one dollar that night. The local TV station KPRC gave away a 102 piece silver set to the fan who drove the farthest, and the largest family in attendance won a TV set. Prizes were also doled out for the youngest, oldest, and heaviest fans in attendance.

Mars fell short of getting a win that night as Ann Laverne won the battle royal against Mars, Mae Young, Ellen Olsen, and Eva Lee, but Mars won the majority of matches in Texas, getting wins against Mae Young, Anne Laverne, and Ellen Olsen.

Mars went into a losing streak when she returned to the Carolinas. Pitted against Ellen Olsen, Mars lost in all the same cities where she'd previously beaten Beverly Lehmer. Mars also tasted defeat at the hands of another long time veteran while making her debut in Missouri. Elvira Snodgrass, also known as Elviry Snodgrass, also known as Cousin Elviry, was born Gutherine Fuller in Varnado, Louisiana. A true country girl, she dreamed of a life beyond the farm despite having married and had a daughter at a very young age. She got her wish in the late 1930s when she joined Billy Wolfe's crew and began working with Mildred Burke, Gladys Gillem, and Mae Weston.

Elvira went by many names before her marriage to fellow wrestler Elmer Snodgrass gave her one that would stick. One of the first names she used was Betty Nichols, and as Betty Nichols, Elvira became the last woman to defeat Mildred Burke head-to-head and win her Women's World Championship in Columbus in 1938. She dropped the title back to Burke just a few weeks later in the same city, but over time, that loss had been swept under the rug to further solidify Burke's status as an unstoppable force.

As one of the most senior members of the women's wrestling sisterhood, Elvira was decidedly old school in working with the new girls. Belle Starr, who trained with Elvira a few years later, laughed when I brought up her name. "She was so rough!"

Mars met up with June Byers, Cora Combs, and Ellen Olsen in Ohio at the end of October to work a series of tag matches. Mars got to play the heel this time, partnering with Byers against Combs and Olsen. From there she hit the road with Ella Waldek, a former roller derby girl and semi-pro softball player from Custer, Washington. As a teenager, Waldek worked with a test group on bombers during World War II and survived a plane crash during a test flight that left her badly burned. Mars and Ella finished out the month of November battling their way across Tennessee, Louisiana, and Alabama. Waldek took the villain's role, smacking Mars and the referees around every night.

Mars finished out the year working against June Byers. The ladies picked up their feud in Tennessee and traveled through Arkansas, Oklahoma, Texas, and Missouri. While the girls were working almost every night, women's matches were a rare treat in many of the towns they visited. They often appeared in the semi-main event, working two-out-of-three falls, and promoters knew they could count on the ladies to pack the house, even if the names weren't familiar.

Mars lost to June Byers in Oklahoma City on December 22, two days before Christmas. It's not clear if she had time to return home to Detroit for Christmas, but the following day, she appeared at the Columbia Gym in Louisville, Kentucky. Matchmaker Francis McDonogh announced just before the holiday that Mildred Burke would be returning on January 30, and a women's tag match would help decide who would be her challenger.

The tag bout placed Mars on the "Yankee" team along with Ella Waldek. Waldek was certainly a Northerner being from Washington state, but for the purposes of the match, McDonogh advertised her as a native of New Jersey. Their opponents, the "Southern" team, included Texan June Byers and Florida girl Dottie Dotson. Mars and Ella fell short in their efforts to defeat the Southern team and thus missed out on being considered for a title shot with Mildred Burke.

Top: Mars spins trainer Lou Leonard over her shoulders. Bottom: Lou Leonard looks on as Marie Gallagher works Mars over. (Courtesy Marcella Foreit Robinette.)

Beauty Parade magazine 1948.

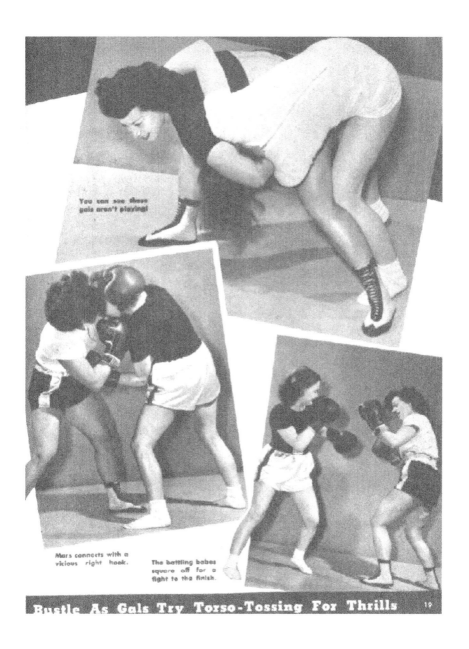

You can see these gals aren't playing!

Mars connects with a vicious right hook.

The battling babes square off for a fight to the finish.

Bustle As Gals Try Torso-Tossing For Thrills 19

41

Hit! magazine 1948.

NOTE: MARIE ISN'T FOOLING. SHE'S REALLY PUTTING ON PRESSURE.

NOW ART DIRECTOR LAMAR'S GOT HER IN THE AIR AGAIN!

WHO WON? LEONARD WAS SMART. HE CALLED IT A DRAW.

Mars with actress Mary Beth Hughes. (Courtesy Marcella Foreit Robinette.)

Peter Lind Hayes, Mars, and Mary Healy. (Courtesy Marcella Foreit Robinette.)

MILDRED BURKE WORLDS CHAMPION WRESTLER
AND SON JOE

Top: Mars demonstrates her strength with Lou Leonard. Bottom: Women's World Champion Mildred Burke and her son Joe.

Mars flexes for the camera.

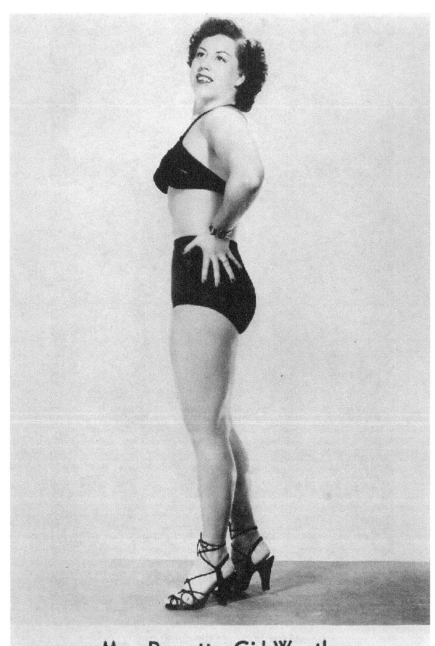

Mars Bennett - Girl Wrestler

Early promo photo of Mars Bennett.

As 1951 began, Mars traveled to Texas along with Cora Combs, Millie Stafford, and Nell Stewart. Mars and Nell were no strangers. The two had faced off on a few occasions in 1950, but this marked the first time Mars and the popular veteran had worked a circuit together.

Born in Birmingham, Alabama, the beautiful, blonde Stewart broke into the business in 1944. Stewart became a favorite of Billy Wolfe as well as the fans, and she was one of a number of ladies to have an affair with the boss.

Wolfe often used sex as a means to control the women under his employ. If you did what he asked, you would get better bookings and better pay days. Refuse, and your pay would suffer. Wolfe also kept control by taking 40% of everyone's pay, keeping Burke distanced and isolated from the other ladies, and pitting the women against one another - sometimes just for his own amusement.

Sadly, Mars was no exempt from such treatment. In notes written by Mildred Burke that later formed the foundation of her biography *Queen of the Ring* by Jeff Leen, the champ wrote about walking into a hotel room and seeing Mars on the ground with Mae Young in the midst of a vicious fight. Wolfe had not only started the fight, he stood by and watched as two of his stars clawed at one another.

Lily Bitter was initially advertised for the Texas tour, but Cora Combs took her place on those cards. Also on hand was Mae Young, who acted as a special guest referee in the January 9, 1951 bout that took place at the Fair Park Coliseum in Paris, Texas.

The ladies stole the show in Paris with Mars playing the heel and roughhousing Cora Combs all over the ring. Mae Young warned Mars repeatedly to let up, and when Mars refused, Mae disqualified her. Mars protested the decision vociferously, but Cora Combs grabbed her from behind, allowing Mae to sock her with a left hook that sent Mars sprawling outside the ring.

Two days later, the ladies stole the spotlight from the boys in Galveston with a tag match and two singles bouts. Mars defeated Cora Combs in her singles match and then tagged up with Millie Stafford to defeat Combs and the Texas Women's Champion Nell Stewart.

Mars defeated Nell Stewart the following night at the City Auditorium in Houston, Texas, winning the Texas Women's Championship. Four nights later, Mars was once again the challenger as she faced Champion Nell Stewart at the Sportatorium in Dallas. Mars won again, winning the Texas Women's Championship again. The cities were spread far apart enough that wrestling results didn't travel between the two, allowing Mars to win the title not once but twice from Nell Stewart on the same loop.

Sadly, Mars didn't get much of a chance to carry the title, as Nell defeated her in Houston on the 19th to reclaim her Texas crown. There was no second rematch in Dallas because the ladies had to leave the mild January weather of Texas and headed due north to the frozen regions of Minnesota, Wisconsin, and North Dakota.

The endless travel was nothing new to Mars. She'd been on the road with the circus for years. But Mars spent her circus winters in Sarasota learning new skills, staying fit, and enjoying the Florida weather. Traveling to the Dakotas in the dead of winter had to be a shock!

After working a series of matches against Nell Stewart and then Cora Combs, Mars headed to the even colder weather of Alberta, Canada to work for Stu Hart, the legendary wrestler, promoter, trainer, and patriarch of the Hart Family Dynasty. A crowd of 7000 packed the Stampede Corral in Calgary on February 15 to see Mars come from behind and win two falls to one against Millie Stafford.

A smaller crowd of 1500 turned out the following night in Lethbridge, Ontario. Stafford drew the ire of the fans playing heel, and *The Lethbridge Herald* declared her to be twice as mean-spirited as the male heels on the card. Four days later in Edmonton, more than 3000 fans were turned away as a capacity crowd of 4000 watched Mars pick up yet another win over Millie.

Mars headed South at the end of February and found herself in Lincoln, Nebraska, where she teamed up with Syrian grappler Sheba Zenni to wrestle Ann Stanley and Mae Young at the Fairgrounds Arena. Writing in *The Lincoln Star*, sports editor Norris Anderson sang the praises not of the ladies but a former All-American football player named Tom Novak whose job it was to call the ladies match.

"A brute of a man, [Novak] has faced every force known to sportdom. He has flung his stocky frame against... the toughest linemen in college football. Tom Novak is a man and then some. Physically, he can take care of himself against any given adversary at any given time.

We'd bet on that with a single exception. These feminine wrestlers, once their dander is up, are the toughest problem Tom has faced in his 25 years."

Yes, it seems Tom Novak had some difficulty containing the action in the tag bout between the four ladies. He kept things largely under control for one fall, but during the second, things spiraled out of control. "It ended with the foursome flooring this brute of a man in as wild a finish as you'll see in wrestling."

Novak may have taken some bumps for the ladies, but Anderson concluded his coverage by assuring readers that Novak is, first and foremost, a gentleman. Tom could have tossed all four ladies into the rafters if he wanted, but he would never strike a lady!

Mars made a loop through the Midwest, wrestling in Iowa, Minnesota, and Ohio before heading to Pennsylvania. She skipped right past her home state of Michigan, and in fact never had the opportunity to wrestle there. Women's wrestling was banned at the time in Michigan, so Mars never had the chance to wrestle in her home town of Detroit.

Mars had a chance to return to her adopted home state of Florida at the end of March. The Sunshine State tour kicked off with a visit to Sarasota, winter home of the Ringling Brothers circus, where Mars scored a victory over Cora Combs. Local papers not only hailed her as a former member of the circus but billed her correctly as a native of Detroit thanks to a new nickname: The Detroit Devastator.

The girls turned north in mid-March, working New Jersey, Pennsylvania, Maryland, D.C., and Ohio through the spring. She continued her singles feud with Cora Combs while also battling it out with Millie Stafford, Beverly Lehmer, and Carol Cook. More and more promoters were featuring the girls on television, and Mars found herself in a featured TV match against Carol Cook when the ladies visited Baltimore on April 3. The TV show broadcast on WMAR went live at 10 p.m. from the Coliseum, and fans who tuned in saw Carol Cook get the best of Mars in the match.

Mars also spent a lot of time in the ring with Nell Stewart as tag partners, and the combination of the hot headed redhead and the blonde bombshell proved to be good business. "These team matches between women wrestlers are action-packed from start to finish," said Bert Bertolini, the matchmaker in Wilmington, Delaware. "The fans like to see fast action, and the women, quick to grasp the situation, provide it."

So popular were the ladies, they carried almost an entire show at Dover's Memorial Hall in Ohio on April 16. Cora Combs defeated

Beverly Lehmer in the opener followed by Mars Bennett topping Millie Stafford in the second. The third match, a "dull, drawn-out affair," saw Chief Lone Eagle defeat Frankie Talaber in two straight falls, the second by disqualification. The girls helped everyone forget the snooze-fest between Talaber and Eagle with a slam-bang main event tag bout.

Cora Combs and Mars Bennett teamed up against Millie Stafford and Beverly Lehmer in a two-out-of-three falls battle that left the near-capacity crowd of 1500 hoarse with excitement. The match went to three falls, with Combs and Bennett getting the victory, and Referee Scarpuzzi had his hands full throughout. All four ladies ended up in the ring on several occasions, and Scarpuzzi took a scissor hold around the neck at one point as he vainly tried to keep order.

Despite their popularity with wrestling fans and the promoters who profited from them, a few newspaper notices from this time reveal the long road lady wrestlers and women in general had ahead to earn equal respect. Prior to a bout between Cora Combs and Mars Bennett, Pittsburgh sports editor Al Abrams acknowledged that the ladies knew "all the tricks of the game plus some their brother grapplers don't know," but just had to add, "They're entertaining, but this department still hews to the line that the show belongs on the stage and not the sports arenas."

The Boston Globe also ran a photo of Mars and Nell Stewart, dressed in their lady-like finest, posing with a Boston traffic officer and a Chamber of Commerce member in a promotion for the Chamber's clean-up, fix-up campaign. Nell and Mars are depicted as showing the traffic officer the correct way to use a broom.

It's hard to imagine modern lady grapplers like Thunder Rosa or Sasha Banks posing in dresses and demonstrating the proper way to use household cleaning equipment. But the ladies likely handled these moments with as much humor as grace. Yes, they were being forced to pose in traditional domestic roles, but Mars and Nell were Billy Wolfe protégés. They could have twisted traffic officer Tom Wilson and Chamber Chairman J. Ralph Stout into human pretzels if they wished!

Mars cross-crossed the country over the summer, working from New Jersey to Utah and dozens of points in between. She spent a good deal of time in the Midwest feuding with Dot Dotson, a former bus driver and cab driver who spun an incredible story about how she became a pro wrestler.

Dotson was behind the wheel of her cab in Orlando one evening when a big bruiser of a man asked for a ride to Daytona Beach, far outside her usual territory. Dotson drove the man to his requested destination, but when she tried to collect her fare, the man assaulted her. Dotson hit the man with a right hand to the chin that sent him to the ground but only for a moment. The man got back on his feet and came at her again.

Dotson used the man's momentum to toss him over her shoulders just as another car was passing by. The driver, a man, asked if she wanted help. Dotson told the man no, she didn't. She hit her attacker with a left hook and then slammed him over her shoulders again, knocking him out.

The man in the other car waited with Dotson for the police, who carted the unruly passenger off to jail. He then gave Dotson a business card that read, "Phil Duffy, Wrestling Promoter, Lakeland, Florida." And the rest, as they say, is history.

Mars played second fiddle to Lily Bitter in the August, 1951 issue of *Official Wrestling* magazine. Mars was portrayed as a long time top girl in the business in the article, but it's Lily who takes the spotlight.

"Unlike most young wrestling aspirants, she did not require weeks or months of training before making her pro debut." Lily, the article said, wrestled her first match just ten days after approaching Willie Gilzenberg, manager of Tony Galento and co-founder of the World Wide Wrestling Federation, and saying she wanted to wrestle.

"She shows more promise at this stage of the fame than did Champion Mildred Burke," says Billy Wolfe in the story. "In a year she will be one of the most polished wrestlers in the sport." Mars is pictured dealing out a great deal of punishment to Lily before Lily turned the tables and claimed victory.

Mars was in Missouri preparing to tangle with Cora Combs when tragedy struck the ladies' ranks on July 27. Mae Young and Ella Waldek were in East Liverpool, Ohio that night to work with Eva Lee and eighteen year old Janet Wolfe, the recently adopted daughter of Billy Wolfe. The teenage Wolfe took a hard body slam from Ella Waldek during the second match of the night, a seven minute affair that ended with a loss for Wolfe. She complained of headaches in the locker room but still made her way back to the ring to team up with Eva Lee against Waldek and Mae Young. Not long into the bout, Wolfe tagged Lee in and then collapsed on the ring apron.

Wolfe received medical attention at ringside before being rushed to the hospital. She never regained consciousness and died at the hospital. Her death was ruled an accident, and Waldek was never charged. The incident sent shockwaves throughout the professional wrestling community, especially with the ladies.

Mars worked in East Liverpool, Ohio on October 27, exactly three months after Janet Wolfe's death. She also worked with Mae, Eva, and Ella in the months following the accident, including several tag matches that featured Mae, Eva, and "The Nature Girl" Adele Antone in Ohio. Mars and Adele also competed in a mixed tag match in Marietta, Georgia, where Adele partnered with Red Dugan and Mars teamed with "Honey Boy" Hannegan.

Mars faced a few new challengers in addition to Adele Antone that fall. Ida Mae Martinez was a teenage runaway who became a country singer and yodeler before turning to wrestling.

Ida Mae's first ever match was against Mars, and she spoke about that encounter in the documentary *Lipstick and Dynamite*. "[She] scared me to death. When she hit me, I knew it. So of course she beat me. My heart must have been pounding!"

Donna Marie Dieckman was a native of Cleveland who quickly became a fan favorite in Ohio. She fell in love with pro wrestling when her father took her to the matches as a young girl, and she followed her dream to become a wrestler herself. Donna, Ida Mae, and Adele became regular opponents for Mars throughout the fall of 1951 as the ladies traveled the Midwest and the East Coast.

On September 8, 1951, Mars made an appearance on *Inside Bob and Ray*, a radio program hosted by the popular comedy duo of Bob Elliot and Ray Goulding. Bob and Ray were known for their dry comedic banter, and Elliot was the father of comedian Chris Elliot. The national radio broadcast put Mars in the spotlight as Bob and Ray interviewed her about her career as a lady wrestler.

Mars finished the year 1951 working shows in West Texas, New Mexico, and Arizona beginning the week before Christmas. She had a match in Abilene on Christmas Eve against Carol Cook. Mars and Carol spent Christmas day away from home in the great state of Texas and locked up again on December 26 in Lubbock. They also wrestled in Amarillo and Odessa before heading to Arizona, where they rang in the New Year with a number of their fellow lady wrestlers working battle royals.

The first took place on New Year's Eve, December 31, in Phoenix and featured Mars, Cora Combs, Dot Dotson, Helen Collins, and Lorraine Johnson. The next day, the ladies were joined by Nell Stewart and Carol Cook for a seven-woman battle royal in El Paso won by Stewart.

They did it again the next night in Tucson in front of a record-breaking crowd of 2700 fans. The Tucson match came with an added stipulation: the last two ladies standing would face off in a singles match. Carol Cook and Nell Stewart won the battle royal that night, with Mars being the last lady eliminated. Stewart won the head to head battle against Cook.

The rules for these battle royals varied. Some went until only one woman was left standing. Some lasted until two women were left, with those two women fighting a singles match. In another variation, five ladies would start the battle royal. The first one pinned would be done for the night. The second and third girls eliminated would face each other in a singles match. Then the last two women standing would wrestle in another singles bout. In yet another variation, the last four women to survive would pair off for a tag team match.

The battle royals were a fun spectacle for the fans, but having multiple girls in the ring increased the risk for injury. Ida Mae came out of one battle royal with Mars feeling worse for wear. "Mars Bennett stomped my ribs one night in Kansas City. You could hear them snap."

The biggest losers on battle royal nights were the men. The ladies prided themselves on their ability to steal the show every night, no matter who else was on the card. They often did so with their singles and tag marches, and the battle royals were always crowd pleasers.

Mars and Cora Combs flew across the southern border in mid-January to wrestle in a number of cities in Mexico. The ladies appeared in the main event on a majority of the cards and drew a great deal of press with their appearance. Mars and Cora took full advantage of the moment as well, seeing the sights in Veracruz and other destinations. The girls returned to action in the Southwestern U.S. at the end of the month, competing in singles matches as well as tag team bouts with Carol Cook and Lorraine Johnson,

Mars got a very brief taste of the winter cold in early February when she bounced up to north to wrestle in Boston, Massachusetts, and Anderson, Indiana. Then it was off to Texas, where Mars spent the rest of February duking it out with Millie Stafford. One show in Fort Worth saw Mars and Millie working the semi-main event underneath Duke Keomuke and the World Heavyweight Champion Lou Thesz, but the real story of that event took place in the opener. The show opened with a pair of trailblazers squaring off: African American grapplers Ethel Johnson and Louise Green.

Mars returned to Mexico in the spring along with Violet Viann, Ruth Boatcallie, and Jean Kennedy. As if two women's matches weren't enough to draw the fans, the ladies were joined by four of the most popular midget wrestlers of the day: Tiny Roe, Tom Thumb, Farmer Peter, and Pee Wee James. As with her previous trip, Mars took plenty of pictures of the sights and her tour mates, and everyone soaked up the sun poolside.

Mars also wrestled and partied in Cuba that year. A business card from the famous Copacabana made its way into her scrapbook, along with a photo of Mars sharing a booth with three handsome young men.

It was right after one of Mars's Mexico trips that her fox terrier made headlines. Blondie traveled with Mars from New York to Tucson, but when Mars left for Mexico, she had to leave her best pal behind. Mars left her in the care of Dottie Dotson, who was in Arizona at the time.

Dotson was unable to remain in Arizona until Mars returned from Mexico, so Blondie traveled with Dotson to Omaha, Nebraska. Dotson's next stop was Tampa, but rather than take the dog to Florida, she stopped in Birmingham, Alabama, and had Blonde sent via express to Adele Antone in Houston. Texas.

Mars called Adele from El Paso, and Adela offered to ship Blondie to Mars. Mars told Adela to hold off. She'd drive to Houston herself to pick her precious pooch up. But when Mars arrived at Adele's house, Blondie was gone!

Adele had gotten into an argument with an "ice man from Columbus" the night before. Adele had stepped out of the apartment for a moment to cool off. When she returned, the ice man and Blondie had vanished.

Dot Dotson was called. The police were called. Mars poured her heart out to Officer J.H. Robbins. The Houston Police sent word out, and a search began for the missing dog. Mars saved the newspaper clipping about the police report and the APB. She left no other records behind about the case of her missing fox terrier, so sadly, the story has no resolution. As a dog lover, I like to think Mars did reunite with her beloved Blondie.

Mars returned to Georgia in May of 1952 and worked a few more mixed gender tag matches. She partnered with Riot Squad member Danny Dusek to wrestle Millie Stafford and Don McIntyre in Columbus. Millie changed partners in Augusta four days later, taking Angelo Martinelli to the ring in her attempt to defeat Mars and Danny Dusek.

Mars clearly enjoyed the mixed tag affairs because in June, she and Ida Mae Martinez participated in a few more down in Louisiana. Martinez and Rex Mobley defeated Mars and Jack Kelly in Shreveport. Charlie Ray and Martinez defeated Mars and The Big Scot in Monroe.

Mars was two years in and a veteran by this point, but new ladies continued to step into the ring, including Ella Phillips of Houston, Mary Jane Mull of Toledo, Lynn Livingston of New York, and Ruth Boatcallie of Bryan, Texas. Demand for girl wrestlers was soaring, and Billy Wolfe continued to expand his offerings, even as behind the scenes things fell apart with his star attraction.

The marriage of Billy Wolfe and Mildred Burke was finally reaching the breaking point. The couple kept up appearances in the public eye as long as they could, but by 1952 the foundation had crumbled too far. Over the next two years, Wolfe and Burke would battle behind the scenes for control of the women's wrestling empire they had built together.

The women's ranks suffered another blow on June 22, 1952. Elvira Snodgrass was driving alone outside Florence, Kentucky when her car rolled off the road into a ditch. Elvira survived the crash, but the injuries she sustained in the accident would end her career. According to family lore, Elvira had the driver's window down and her arm outside the car when the accident took place. Her arm was pinned between the door and the ground, and Elvira cut her own arm off to escape. Newspaper reports indicate Elvira had the arm amputated some time after the accident, but both Elvira's niece and nephew, both alive at the time this author wrote Elvira's biography, swore the story was true.

The loss of Elvira, coupled with the behind the scenes turmoil in the Wolfe-Burke household, left a void at the top of the women's division. Promoters and the press were looking for new stars, and Mars Bennett proved she had star power.

Mars appeared in the 1952 edition *The Wrestling Fan's Book*, a publication put out by Sid Feder. Feder described Mars as a villain with a flailing ring style utilizing airplane spins, flying mares, and jaw breakers.

Boxing and Wrestling magazine also ran a story on Mars in their June 1952 issue, just one page away from a feature on a wrestler she'd frequently worked alongside, Lord Leslie Carlton. Charles A. Smith painted a portrait of a confident, strong woman who loved the spotlight.

"I like any type of work that brings me in front of the public," said Mars. "I am excited by... the cheers of a large audience. I seem to wrestle better the larger the crowd is... Not only that, but the applause of the fans makes you want to outdo yourself. You start to think more quickly, clearly. You take care of yourself. Keep yourself in condition and you are encouraged to carry on under all circumstances. You know what I mean, Smithy? The show must go on and all that."

Smith reveals much about Mars as a person in the article. Mars did not drink or smoke. She avoided starches, fried food, and fatty food. "I like steak of course and plenty of salads, fruit, and milk. I always eat a good breakfast, and I like good food."

Smith also shared an anecdote that showed Mars as a lady who could stand toe to toe with the boys in the other locker room. While Smith and Bennett sat behind a closed door enjoying their talk, the walls began to shake as a large man pounded on the door. "Knock it off and come in!" shouted Mars.

One of the boys working that evening's card, whose name Smith chose to leave out, entered the room. The man grabbed Mars by the shoulders and planted a kiss on her cheek. "Hello, honey!" he said.

Mars took hold of the man's wrist and shoved him to one side. "Okay, Columbus, that's enough exploring today."

Mars let go, and Smith noted the grimace of pain on the man's face. "That's some grip you have there."

As she had in the past, Mars sang the praises of Mildred Burke, whom she credited with breaking her into the business. "Frankly, Smithy, I didn't think I'd qualify after my first half dozen bouts, but Mildred Burke was keeping an eye on me and kept telling me I had what it took... that I'd make good. Then I saw Mae Weston and Mildred Burke in a tough match. Mildred was bounced around all over the place but she was biding her time, content to take a beating until Mae Weston relaxed and dropped her guard for that fraction of a second... and when she did, that was enough. In less than a minute the match was all over and Mae had been body slammed into defeat.

"From that day on, I patterned my style after Mildred Burke's."

Remember those words, dear reader.

Mars also talked about some her worst injuries. "June Byers and Mae Young have given me my hardest fights to date. In one match with June, I had to have four stitches put in a cut over my eye. While in a bout with Mae Young, my elbow ligaments were badly torn, and I was out of the game for over a month."

More than anything, Smith seemed to appreciate Mars as a lady without airs, an easy-going person who never knew a stranger. "A real good Joe and as forthright a person as you could ever wish to meet. You sense at once that there's something a little more than ordinary about her as soon as you set eyes on her. Mars has a thick, muscular physique which has lost none of its femininity. She looks hard, tough, and is, but she has a gentle, friendly, winning way that sort of captivates you."

In October Mars was on the East Coast wrestling Juanita Coffman, a veteran who had been in the business since 1945. Mars and Juanita competed in a number of singles matches. Coffman took the heel role in those engagements, but when Mars went back to the Midwest to work with Violet Viann, she wore the black hat.

"Mars has little respect for the official rule book," declared *The La Crosse Tribune's* Report on Sports on November 9, "And when and if necessary, she will resort to slightly shady tactics to attain her end - defeating her opponent."

The stakes were raised when Violet and Mars took on tag partners. Carol Cook sided with Violet while Ruth Boatcallie joined forces with Mars. The fans in La Crosse, Wisconsin, joined in the fun by pelting Mars and Ruth with objects thrown into the ring. One fan attempted to toss a chair at the ladies but struck a police officer instead.

The fan was escorted from the building while the remaining fans got to see Mars and Ruth get their comeuppance.

Mars in the ring. (Courtesy Marcella Foreit Robinette.)

Top left: Mars with Carol Cook and Violet Viann. (From the Ruth Boatcallie collection, courtesy Chris Bergstrom.) Top right: Ruth Boatcallie and Mars. Bottom: Living it up in Cuba. (Courtesy Marcella Foreit Robinette.)

Cartoon caricatures of Cora Combs and Mars from their tour of Mexico in 1952. (Courtesy Marcella Foreit Robinette.)

Top: Mars showing off on the beach. Bottom: Sun bathing with Millie Stafford (left) and ready to rumble (right). (Courtesy Marcella Foreit Robinette.)

Mars worked a few battle royals in late November, sharing the ring with Carol Cook, Ruth Boatcallie, Violet Viann, Cora Combs, Carol Carota, Donna Marie Dieckman, Dot Dotson, and a few others in the Tennessee and Arkansas territory. She worked Oklahoma and Texas for most of December, but she found herself back in Georgia before and after Christmas wrestling Violet Viann. Mars and Violet also rang in the New Year together, wrestling in Virginia, the Carolinas, and Florida. Matchmaker Cowboy Luttrall made the ladies the star attraction in the Sunshine State, hyping them both as veteran grapplers who had their sights set on the Women's World Championship still secured around the waist of Mildred Burke.

Mars and Violet were joined by Dot Dotson and Helen Hild, an Omaha, Nebraska, native who ignored her mother's advice to go into the restaurant business to make quick money in professional wrestling. Helen had a son with singer Ted Willis in 1954. She later married "Iron Mike" DiBiase, and her son Theodore would adopt Iron Mike's last name as his own when he became Ted DiBiase. Lynn Livingston, niece of the legendary Cora Livingston, and Theresa Theis, a former ice skating champion from Minnesota, joined the ladies in mid-January for some six-woman battle royals.

Mars had a visitor in the dressing room one night in Orlando. Jack Dempsey stopped in to say hello with his daughter Joan in tow. Writing in the *Orlando Evening Star*, columnist Harry Robarts bore witness to the scene as Mars kicked back with Dempsey and Dot Dotson swapping stories about days gone by.

"You know this guy talked me into the wrestling business," Mars said to Harry and Dot.

"And you've never regretted getting into wrestling, have you?" said Dempsey. Mars agreed, she had not.

Robarts noted that Mars was all smiles sitting next to Dot Dotson, whose hair she tore out later that evening while acquiring a new batch of haters among the Orlando wrestling fans. "Not a touch of the villain which she played so actively on the mat," quipped Robarts.

Dempsey stepped into the ring later that night and decked British wrestler Jack Wentworth to the delight of the record 1657 fans on hand. Yet Robarts says it was the ladies who stole the show. "Mars, who's short as a fence post, and Dot, the world's most famous taxi driver, took over, and frankly, I enjoyed their performance more than the he-males. Those muscles are real, too. They leaned against me once during the picture-posing in the dressing room, which I slyly left out of the early paragraphs, and believe me they're solid."

Kudos to Robarts for not only putting the ladies over, but breaking kayfabe without breaking kayfabe.

On February 9, Mars went to Tampa to take on the Florida Women's Champion, Betty Jo Hawkins. A native of Ashland, Kentucky, Hawkins began wrestling at the age of 20 in 1951. Three years prior to her debut she was an invalid, bed-ridden and battling it out with Polio. Hawkins beat the disease and worked hard to regain her good health. She exceeded everyone's expectations.

Hawkins was taller than Mars at 5'5" with brown hair and blue eyes, and she certainly matched Mars in star power. The stage was set for a clash in Tampa, Florida on February 9 for the Florida Championship. The ladies went on first in a show headlined by the Heavyweight Champion of the World, Lou Thesz. Thesz retained his title against The Great Togo, but Betty Hawkins lost her title defense in just eleven minutes. It only took one fall for Mars Bennett to become the Florida Women's Champion!

A week later, Mars finally got her shot at the biggest prize in the business. Mildred Burke made her way to the Sunshine State in Florida, and as the Florida Champion, Mars was in line to get a shot at the World Championship. Mars had often drawn comparisons to Burke. They were of similar height and similar build, and many believed the two looked alike. The photos printed side by side in the Fort Lauderdale news with similar tops and bottoms make the two ladies look almost like sisters. They even shared the same initials, M.B. Mildred Burke had not lost a singles match in fifteen years. Yes, she claimed to have gone undefeated in seventeen years, but as was already mentioned in this book, she did lose the title briefly to Betty Nichols, aka Elvira Snodgrass, in December of 1938. But Burke's time in the spotlight was quickly coming to an end as the fight between Burke and Billy Wolfe for control of the women's wrestling game continued behind the scenes.

Burke was still the champion in the winter of 1953 and the standard-bearer for all lady wrestlers. Five years after encouraging Mars to try the wrestling game, the champ would meet the circus girl head to head in front of the fans.

Their first confrontation took place on February 18 in St. Petersburg. Mars lost the first fall in seventeen minutes via disqualification. Burke pinned Mars in fifteen minutes to win in straight falls. The next night in Fort Lauderdale, the results were much the same. Mars was disqualified in the first fall for pulling Burke's hair, and Burke tied Mars in knots to win the second fall.

Mars switched from challenger to defender overnight, meeting young Gloria Barratini in Bradenton, Florida to defend her own Florida Women's Championship. A native of Baltimore, Maryland, Barratini was an opera singer before she decided to step into the ring. The ladies went head to head in a number of Florida towns to wrap up February with Mars defeated Barratini in Bradenton, but a few weeks later, the two ladies met again in Tampa. A crowd of 1700 fans cheered as Barratini pinned Mars for the title.

BELLE

Shortly after dropping the Florida Championship to Gloria Barratini, Mars headed north to New England. *The Boston Globe* notes that on February 10, she was on the winning end of a tag team bout against Lynn Livingston and Donna Diekman. The girl in Mars's corner that night was yet another rookie, a native of Ohio named Belle Drummond.

Norma Jean Belle Drummond was six years younger than Mars, born in 1928. An athletically gifted young woman, the Chester, Ohio native became captain of the basketball, softball, and hockey teams at her high school. She also did track and field and set the school record in the girls' long jump.

"I found out in later years that my mom had been molested by her father," says Mars Belle Drummond, Belle's daughter. "I think she may have turned to sports because it was a way to get her anger out."

Belle almost went professional in a different sport. The All-American Girl's Professional Baseball League was still in operation after World War II, and Belle got an offer to play first base for the Fort Wayne Daisies. The team offered her $175 a week plus expenses, which was great money in those days. But before Belle signed her contract, she saw an ad in the Columbus paper posted by Billy Wolfe looking for lady wrestlers.

"I was intrigued," she said years later in an interview. "It was something I wanted to do."

Belle was working in a factory at the time. She went down to Billy Wolfe's gym so he could get a look at her. Wolfe liked what he saw, and Belle began training alongside male wrestlers at his gym. Belle was 5'5" and 150 pounds with bleached blonde hair, drawing comparisons to Jean Harlow if Harlow had put some time in a weight room.

Belle told her daughter that her first match in front of a crowd was against Mars. The earliest advertised match featuring Mars and Belle was actually a tag match, but it's likely this one on one confrontation took place in a carnival tent, the same place where Mars, Mildred Burke, and the majority of lady wrestlers started out. Mars won the match in just three minutes. The veteran was impressed with the rookie's raw talent. They soon became best friends, roommates, and travel partners.

Belle didn't even tell her family when she signed on with Billy Wolfe. Her mother found out one day while she was watching TV with Belle's younger sister Peggy. A wrestling program came on, and Belle's mom was shocked to see her daughter in the ring. Peggy related the story to Belle's daughter years later, recalling how Belle's mother screamed, "Oh my gosh, she's gonna get killed in there!"

Belle's mother put Peggy on a Greyhound bus and sent her off to intercept Belle. She was determined to keep her daughter out of that dangerous business. Peggy quickly got caught up in the excitement. She stayed on the road with her sister and Mars, not as a wrestler but as a driver.

Peggy was only thirteen or fourteen at the time, too young to drive legally even in that time, but she did it anyway. She amassed quite a collection of autographed photos from the wrestlers she met, men and women. She also loved being on the road watching her sister perform.

Belle smoked Swisher Sweets Cigars, which she said helped her stay awake between matches. She never gave the habit up according to Mars Belle, who never did like the smell of them. "I learned not to smoke from her because I hated the smell so bad!"

Even though she was blonde and pretty, Belle Drummond preferred working as a heel. She enjoyed using dirty tactics more than the "clean" style of wrestling, and she loved the heat she got from the crowd. She didn't care so much for the "Hat Pin Marys" who sat at ringside, the little old ladies who on occasion would try to stick her with their hat pins and other makeshift weapons as Belle and Mars walked by.

One night in Cuba, a Hat Pin Mary struck Mars on the head with a high-heeled shoe. Belle was still in her robe and had a pair of brass knuckles in her pocket. She slipped her fingers into the knuckles and struck the woman in the face, knocking four teeth out.

Mars returned home to Florida in late March along with Belle Drummond, Dot Dotson, Ethel Brown, Helen Hild, Mae Young, Gloria Barratini, and Barbara Baker. They paired off for a few singles clashes, but the big draw once again was the battle royal. Mars and Mae were both hailed as former Florida Women's Champions gunning for the title still held by Gloria Barratini.

Mars missed a battle royal on April 6 in Tampa due to a mishap before the match. She got her finger caught in a car door earlier that day and had to bow out. Ironically, Danny Dusek canceled off the same show after being injured in a car accident on the way to the show. *The Tampa Tribune* covered the show under the grim headline "Barattini and Cars Are Winners in Wrestling Bouts."

Mars didn't work the rest of April. It's an assumption to think she took time off to heal her injured hand, but it's certainly plausible. She was advertised for a few more battle royals, but it's not until May we see any new results in the newspapers for her.

Mars was right back in the main event that month when she faced the embattled, long-reigning champion Mildred Burke. Burke was still the recognized world champion, but while a ladies championship match was big news to the locals, Burlington, Vermont was a far cry from the big cities Burke was used to working.

"Mildred Burke is going to land on Mars," declared the *Burlington Daily News* in advance of the big bout. Promoter Jack O'Brien hyped both Mars and Mildred, both of whom had been big draws in the past. "They'll match holds, bites, kicks, hair yanks, etc. over the two-out-of-three falls route," declared the same Burlington sports writer.

The match garnered a great deal of press in the lead up to the event, but the results were not even published in the *Burlington Daily News*. Not that there's any doubt about the conclusion. Burke retained her title, one way or another, and would remain the undisputed women's champion until her controversial title match with June Byers a year later. But Burke's star was already beginning to fade, and with it, the grip she and Billy Wolfe held on women's wrestling was starting to slip.

The war between Mildred Burke and Billy Wolfe intensified behind the scenes. The end of their marriage also brought the end of their business partnership, and one of the biggest questions to be answered was who would retain control of their women's wrestling empire.

While both Wolfe and Burke had plans to maintain their virtual monopoly on women's wrestling, the dispute between Burke and Wolfe created an opportunity for others who had been longing to grab a piece of the women's wrestling action. Among those willing to take advantage was one of the most colorful characters in the history of the business, Jack Pfefer.

Jack Pfefer was born near Warsaw in modern Poland, then under control of Russia. A Jew, Pfefer fled the country by hiding in the boiler room of a ship bound for the United States in 1921. Pfefer worked as a theatrical manager when he first arrived in the US, but within a few short years, he moved into professional wrestling.

Pfefer became infamous for exposing the business as a work after becoming ostracized by the business. He never recanted his stance that wrestling was more entertainment than sport, but he also never left the business. He was very much ahead of his time, for better or worse, because he treated wrestling as an entertainment more than a sport, using special attractions and colorful characters to sell tickets rather than marquee match ups.

Pfefer had an ambitious young woman who was more than willing to help him challenge Wolfe and Burke. Lillian Ellison began her career as a part of Wolfe's stable based in Columbus, but she quit in anger when Wolfe refused to let her take a little time off and attend her father's funeral. To say she had a grudge against Wolfe is putting it mildly.

Pfefer transformed Ellison into Slave Girl Moolah and made her a valet for Tony Olivas, better known as Elephant Boy. Moolah would drop the "slave girl" moniker as she began wrestling on her own, becoming The Fabulous Moolah.

Billy Wolfe had long kept a stranglehold on women's wrestling. If you were a woman and wanted to get booked, you had to go through Wolfe. By mid-1953 Pfefer and Moolah were starting to make some moves.

Moolah was feuding in Texas with the bubble gum-popping hillbilly Daisy Mae that July, and after a series of singles matches, the ladies came back for a tag bout. Daisy Mae chose Darling Dagmar to be her tag partner in a few cities, with Red Tigress filling in elsewhere. Moolah joined forces with a lady named Rosita Rogers.

Mars Belle Drummond has a photo of Rosita in her collection, and one look at the photo will tell you why. It's Mars Bennett! Mars worked as both Rosita Rogers and Verne Bottoms, another name that, like Darling Dagmar, was later given to a different lady wrestler.

Pfefer was known for playing the name game, creating names that sounded a lot like the top stars of the day in order to sell more tickets. Hobo Brazil, Bruno Sanmartino, and Lou Fez were just some of the attractions Jack Pfefer promoted over the years. In fact some of the male headliners on the cards with Rosita Rogers that summer included "Mr. America" (not Gene Stanlee), "Nature Boy" Tommy Phelps, "Gorgeous George" Baron, and Argentina Zuma, who was pictured doing the splits like the much more famous Argentina Rocca.

Mars may very well have been covering her tracks by changing names when she changed bosses. Billy Wolfe was chums with most of the territorial promoters. One phone call from him, and Mars Bennett would be finished. But Rosita Rogers? She never worked for Billy Wolfe. She was someone new, someone exciting. With no internet or national TV coverage, Mars could easily keep a low profile by changing names. Rosita Rogers was billed as a newcomer. No hometown, no home state, and no biography was given for her, so it certainly seems she was trying not to attract undue attention!

It's also unclear how or why Mars chose to jump ship and work for Jack Pfefer, but knowing what motivated Mars, the money he offered had to be good. We don't know what Mars was making working for Billy, but thanks to Jack Pfefer, we do know what Mars made working for him. Jack was a meticulous record keeper, and all of his files now reside at the Notre Dame University Library in South Bend, Indiana.

One of those files, marked "Bennett, Mars 1953," that contains several sheets of paper with handwritten accounts of Mars's earnings from the summer of 1953 written letterhead paper from The Baker Hotel in Dallas. The ledgers cover the weeks of July 20 through August 29.

Mars's photo appears in the July 27 paper in Waco with the name Rosita Rogers below. The statement printed below shows how much Mars/Rosita made that week.

Statement Week from July 27, 1953

Monday July 27	Waco	25.00
Tue - 28	Dallas	35.00
Wed - 29	Corpus Christi	35.00
Thur - 30	————————————	
Fridy [sic] - 31	San Antonio	35.00
Sat - Aug 1	Mineral Wells	22.00
		152.00

Received in full payment for above dates.

The page is signed at the bottom: "Mars Bennet."

Mars and Moolah's rival Daisy Mae was an early protégé of Moolah. Daisy Mae, real name Pat Lewis, was the wife of wrestler Frank Robinson, who wrestled as character Hillbilly Stumpy before becoming Farmer Brown. Daisy Mae used to accompany Stumpy to the ring. She would put two sticks of gum in her mouth, and when Stumpy needed an assist, she would blow a bubble as big as her head and pop it in Stumpy's opponent's face to distract them. She lived with Moolah at one point and had a hand in training Moolah's daughter Mary.

The name Darling Dagmar became famous in the 1960s when Moolah gave it to a midget wrestler from North Carolina named Kathy Carlton. Carlton was only eleven years old at the time these tag bouts took place. Sylvia McMillan was the first Darling Dagmar. When Carlton first started wrestling in the 60s, she was often referred to as Little Darling Dagmar.

A week after debuting as Rosita Rogers, Mars dropped the false name and continued working for Pfefer under her own name. She teamed up once again with Moolah to wrestle Daisy Mae and her new partner Red Tigress. The masked woman was another Billy Wolfe trainee Catherine Simpson, also known as Catherine the Great.

Belle Drummond was not far behind Mars in joining Moolah's crew, and like Mars, she tried on a new name. Her new identity stuck a little longer as she became Princess Maritza, the Argentine Bombshell. The Princess became Daisy Mae's new tag partner after Red Tigress. She also faced off with Mars in some singles matches, winning via disqualification when Mars played dirty.

The ladies headlined a show at Casino Arena in Corpus Christi at the end of August with three matches: A singles bout between Moolah and Princess Maritza; another single match between Mars and Daisy Mae; and a five-woman handicap tag match pitting Moolah and Mars against Princess Maritza, Daisy Mae, and Darling Dagmar. Moolah defeated Maritza, and Daisy Mae held Mars to a fifteen minute draw, but even with the three on one advantage, the fan favorites couldn't overcome the dirty tricks of Mars and Moolah.

New England promoters hailed the arrival of Mars in September, advertising her as the girl with the million dollar diamonds. It's noted Mars was a former Ringling Brothers circus performer as well, but it almost seems as if the goal was to create confusion between Mars and the other "MB" Mildred Burke, who was known for wearing large diamonds herself.

The girls traveled north with another signature Jack Pfefer creation Goliath, a long, tall wrestler billed as being seven-foot in Texas and 7'4" in New England. In reality, Frank Hugh McKenzie was about 6'9", and he achieved his greatest success when Pfefer transformed him into the cowboy persona Tex McKenzie. He was a perfect babyface with a humble, "aww shucks" demeanor who became a star in the Detroit and Toronto territories as well as Australia.

Mars wrestled Senorita Leona Cordova of Mexico, a name that appears only a few times in the newspapers of the time. It's likely an alias for another of Moolah's girls at the time. Other rivals include Candy Carrol, Lulu Lamarr, and of course, Princess Maritza. The Princess's photo appears in a few ads alongside Mars, and it's clearly Belle Drummond.

The crowds in New England were much smaller than they had seen in Texas. Only 300 turned out to see "Princess Maritza" defeat Mars in Brattleboro, Vermont. Still, the girls frequently found themselves in the main event, the best paying match on the card, in these tiny towns. Many ads just listed the girls' names as headliners with two or three other matches promised. They even appeared in a few televised matches that boosted ticket sales in small towns across Vermont, New Hampshire, and Maine.

Mars was certainly the biggest name on most of the cards in the Northeast. The Elephant Boy put in a few appearances in these small town New England venues as did Argentina Zuma and the German giant Karl Von Eric, but Jack Pfefer's menagerie of characters could hardly claim the star power and reputation Mars had gained by late 1953.

Mars did everything she could to put her best friend on the map as well. Belle's Princess Maritza was cast as the fresh, eager babyface trying to take down the dastardly circus girl. The more Mars dipped into her bag of dirty tricks, the more fans backed the Argentinian champion. Yes, the Princess was now billed as a champion of her native country, while Mars was billed as a women's champion in "many states." Anything to boost ticket sales.

Maritza and Mars were on opposite sides of the ring in the State Armory in Pittsfield, Massachusetts on Thanksgiving night, November 26, when things really got out of hand. Maritza teamed with Ann Lake while Mars teamed up with Jean Hogan. Hogan was billed as Jean Hagen in one town, a likely tip of the hat of Jack Pfefer's hat that he wanted fans to mistake her for the movie star famous for her turn as Lina Lamont in 1952's *Singin' in the Rain*.

The crowd of 900 ate it up as the ladies threw "everything but the ring posts" at one another. All of the ladies gave as good as they got, but it was referee Jim Taylor who came out the real loser. The Bostonian found himself on the bottom of the pile when all four ladies decided to jump him at the same time.

The main tussle between the girls certainly outshined the semi-final that saw Gorgeous George Grant top Drop Kick Mercier and the opener between Karl Von Eric - not to be confused with Fritz Von Erich - and a cowboy named Jesse James.

JUST LIKE JUNE

Bookings were scarce in the winter of 1954. Mars had only a handful of shows, all frigid in New England, as the year began. Belle Drummond was in the same boat, still wresting as the Argentinian Princess Maritza before small houses in Vermont and Maine. They competed in singles bouts and a few battle royals, but the small houses were not earning them much money. It's no surprised that by March, the ladies returned working for Billy Wolfe.

Traveling back to the Midwest, Mars reunited with old rivals Cora Combs, Dot Dotson, Ethel Brown, and Donna Dieckman while also facing some new foes. China Mira, a Florida girl billed as a native of Cuba, faced Mars in one half of a double main event in Marion, Ohio. The other half of the main event was a tag bout between The Bowery Boys and the African-American duo of Ricky Waldo and his mentor "The Black Panther" Jim Mitchell. Mars and China also had a televised match, appearing live on on Channel 5 in Dayton, Ohio.

Mars returned to Marion as part of a "triple main event." The Bowery Boys had a rematch with Waldo and Mitchell, Bull Montana faced Tarzan Zimba, and Mars faced her best pal Belle. No longer Princess Maritza, Belle was advertised as Belle Drummond - at least in the cities that bothered to get her name right.

The girls made a swing through West Virginia in March, and *The Charleston Daily Mail* sent a reporter named Nancy Kane to get a 'behind the scenes' look at the lady wrestlers on March 13, 1954. As the crowd filed into the Armory, eager to see the excitement women's wrestling, Kane found the ladies relaxed as they prepared themselves in the locker room.

Donna Marie Dieckman answered the door when Kane came knocking. She saw China Mira lounging in a chair talking with Belle Drummond while Mars combed her hair, looking in a mirror. Kane asked if she could get a photo of the four ladies together, but the girls said no. "No pictures together. Makes us look too friendly. Bad publicity."

Kane and Mars chatted briefly about the latter's former career in the circus, and Mars gave the reporter a good reason for the career change. "It's not so far to the ground."

The ladies cast aside their relaxed, friendly demeanor when Mars and China took to the ring. Mars entered first, sneering at the crowd and whipping her cape off with a flourish. As soon as the bell rang, all hell broke loose. Both women threw hard punches, and Mars showed off her tumbling skills as she battered China around the ring. The fans hurled obscenities at Mars and the referee when she scored a pin over China and stole the victory, but they soon settled back into their seats, smoking and devouring their peanuts and drinks.

Belle and Donna were next with Belle taking on the heel role. Fans shouted insults at the blonde with her shiny, red wrestling gear as she locked up with Dieckman, dressed in black and white. The match ended with Belle tossing Dieckman out of the ring. Injured and unable to crawl back under the ropes, Dieckman was declared the loser.

It was too much for a female fan at ringside, who rose to her feet and hurled insults at Belle. "All five feet and 100 pounds quivered with rage and indignation," wrote Nancy Kane. "She screeched abusive remarks and appeared quite willing to continue the match out on the floor. Still complaining, she finally sat down."

The big finale was a tag match, with Donna Marie and China teaming up to seek revenge on Mars and Belle. Kane noted that the ladies were only supposed to be in the ring two at a time, but the referee had his hands full as all four frequently crawled through the ropes to join the action, turning into "screaming, slugging, biting, hair-pulling banshees."

The wilder the action was between the ropes, the more frenetic the crows became. When Donna Marie went down on her back, suffering the final pinball, the crowd lost their minds. Mars and Belle celebrated. China looked with pity on her tag partner as the referee scooped her into his arms to carry her to the back.

"Still complaining loudly, the crowd filed out," said Kane in the wrap up. "Two overwrought females took to the side profanely accusing the referee of highly unethical, undesirable, and immoral practices. In contrast, the women wrestlers seemed pretty tame. Maybe they had the wrong ones in the ring?"

Belle joined Mars for a few mixed gender matches as winter gave way to spring. In Wisconsin Belle teamed up with George Strong against Mars and Bob Massey. In Ohio Belle and Billy Box took on Mars and

Aztec Garcia. The girls also appeared in all girl tag matches as well as a battle royal during the month of April.

A new rival emerged in late April as Mars began working against eighteen-year old Lee Chona LeClaire. LeClaire was born in West Virginia but billed as a French girl. In 1955 she appeared on the TV show *What's My Line?* A year later, only twenty years old, she married Billy Wolfe, who was then forty years her senior.

Mars and Belle moved on from the Ohio territory in early May. They took the main event slot in Manhattan, Kansas, but they played second fiddle to the boys in Kansas City. Gorgeous George faced Wild Red Berry that night with Jack Dempsey acting as special guest referee.

Belle scored the win over Mars that night, but Mars gained a little extra ink in *The Kansas City Times* thanks to an encounter with Tom Van Meter. A former Golden Gloves boxer, Van Meter was in his twilight years and had worked as the Missouri Athletic Commissioner for many years.

When Mars asked the commissioner to borrow a pen, Van Meter pulled out an attractive ball point pen he had been gifted. "I won it by fighting in the Golden Gloves," he said.

Mars looked the old man up and down and quipped, "In the days when you were fighting, they didn't have ball point pens. As a matter of fact, they didn't have Golden Gloves."

After the swing through the Southwest, where Mars and Belle worked a few tags with Dot Dotson and China Mira, the ladies returned to Ohio. They caused quite a story in Fremont, Ohio at a stag party thrown by the local Yacht Club. Belle teamed up with China Mira to face Mars and Olga Zapeda in a a two-out-of-three falls tag match. Belle and China won the first fall, but after Mars and Olga took the second, things got ugly. All four ladies began brawling. Club member Bob Recktenwald, who arranged the event, was pulled into the melee and tossed around the ring. Referee Art Kolbe suffered the wrath of the girls as well and took some bumps of his own.

The crowd of 500 ate it up, and seeing their fellow Yacht Clubber get knocked around really whipped them into a frenzy. Order was restored, and Belle and China were able to take the deciding fall. The Yacht Club members left happy and satisfied, but one has to wonder how many were grilled by their wives when word of the event appeared in the following morning's paper. Especially Bob Recktenwald!

Mars and Belle helped to close out the season in Mansfield, Ohio on June 16, 1954. Promoter Clete Kauffman, a former wrestler himself, announced that wrestling would be going on hiatus due to the summer heat in the Armory. Belle came out the victor that night in a tag match against Mars and Ella Waldek. She stood tall at the end, her hand raised next to her partner - the new Women's World Champion, June Byers.

Mars faced June a few weeks later at the Warren County Fairgrounds in Lebanon, Ohio, for her World Championship. June won that match as well, retaining her championship.

June had become a claimant to the Women's World Championship after winning a tournament for the crown in 1953, but her claim had an asterisk next to it because she had yet to beat Mildred Burke. Byers was Billy Wolfe's choice to succeed his ex, Mildred Burke, as the standard bearer for women's wrestling, but Burke was not about to relinquish the title without a fight. In fact when the dust settled from their divorce, Burke came out the other end as the sole proprietor of their women's wrestling empire.

Burke initially offered to sell her interest to Wolfe, but Wolfe ended up selling to Burke, giving her sole control of the women's wrestling business. Wolfe also pledged to stay out of the business for five years. Wolfe broke that promise in short order and used his connections within the National Wrestling Alliance to regain control of the women's wrestling group and slowly but surely freeze Burke out of the business.

The matter of the Women's World Championship was ultimately decided on August 20, 1954. Unable to come to an amicable resolution, Wolfe and Burke agreed to put on something not seen for many years in professional wrestling: a legitimate shoot match. There would be no pre-arranged finish, no high-flying maneuvers, no bumps, and no selling between Mildred Burke and June Byers. It was skill on skill in a legitimate wrestling contest.

Byers was younger and bigger than Burke. She was married at the time to Wolfe's son, who also happened to be Mildred Burke's former lover. She had Billy Wolfe in her corner, the man who had taught Burke how to shoot two decades earlier. Burke had the edge when it came to experience and skill, but she also had a bad knee, an injury Byers intended to exploit.

The match was scheduled for two-out-of-three falls. Burke submitted the first fall when Byers took advantage of her injured leg. She believed she could come back and take the next two, but after an hour, the match was called off by the athletic commission. The ring announcer declared that Mildred Burke was still the world champion.

It was an unsatisfying result in many ways. The fans felt cheated. Not only did the match not go to the promised two fall finish, it failed to live up to the hype. The fans, who had no way of knowing this was a real contest, were used to the slam-bang action of worked wrestling matches. They couldn't understand why Burke and Byers were spending so much time on offense that, to their eyes appeared to be just plain boring.

Burke held off Byers and denied her the second fall she needed to lay claim to the championship, but Byers had something more powerful than the facts on her side: Billy Wolfe's influence. Her father-in-law used his connections in the press and the NWA to push the story that Byers had defeated Burke. Byers even contended that Burke left the ring during the second fall, leading the athletic commission to end the match, a claim disputed by Burke's biographer Jeff Leen.

Burke would continue to promote herself as the World Champion, but she slowly found herself squeezed out as promoters sided with Wolfe and Byers. Her reign as the Queen of the Ring ended in controversial fashion, and Burke became an outlaw in the business she helped build. She would train and build her own stable of lady wrestlers over the years, and she introduced women's wrestling to Japan, but her glory days were over.

Getting back to Mars Bennett, she was noticeably absent from the wrestling scene after her title match with June Byers in Mansfield, Ohio. She disappears from the newspaper records in July of 1954, and it appears she did not wrestle for a year and a half.

Mars made a few memories of her own with June Byers in August of 1954. One of her scrapbooks includes a page of photos showing Mars, June, and June's son Billy, aka "Billy Boy," enjoying a day of sun at an Aqua Show. Mars and June are seen relaxing in bikinis while Billy boy flexes his muscles shirtless.

Mars was advertised for a return to the ring on October 22, 1954 against June Byers for the World Championship. The event in St. Joseph, Missouri was a stacked boxing and wrestling card headlined by former World Heavyweight Boxing Champion Joe Louis. It's unclear if Mars was a no-show or if the promoter was misinformed, but Betty Hawkins did the honors for June that night, losing to the new champion in two straight falls that took less than sixteen minutes.

Even though she'd been absent from the ring for almost half a year, *Boxing and Wrestling* magazine ran a second story on Mars in December. Charles A. Smith was the scribe once again, and it appears early on that Smith was using a lot of material he had not been able to use in his previous story on Mars. Smith recycles the story of the male wrestler banging on the locker room door during their interview, telling the story of a man pounding on the locker room door, giving Mars a kiss on the lips, and getting a wrist lock in return as if it was fresh and new.

"Scram, Bobby," said Mars in the new account. "And don't come back until Michelmas, 1980!"

The photos that accompany the article are from the same set taken for the 1952 article. Mars is wearing the same pin-striped single piece wrestling gear, and while her opponent is not identified in the 1954 magazine, it's clearly Lily Bitters, the same opponent she was shown wrestling in 1952.

As he did previously, Smith paints a very human face on Mars. "When you meet her," writes Smith, "You sense at once she has something out of the ordinary. Her physique is thick and muscular, yet has lost none of its feminine lines. She looks tough, but the moment she speaks and smiles, you sense the friendliness beneath the hard shell. Outside the ring she's a lady... and no higher praise can be given her."

Smith compares Mars to two of her more well-known contemporaries, June Byers and Nell Stewart. Byers is friendly, says Smith, but there's something in her beauty that keeps you at arm's length. The same goes for Nell Stewart.

But Mars? "You feel more at home with Mars than you do with the rest of the gal grapplers," says Smith. "[She's] a regular Joe if ever there was one."

Mars had a way of putting people at ease. "With Mars Bennett, you are with one of the boys. She can cuss with you, drink a few steins of brew with you, and talk the usual man talk. She's not even above demonstrating her favorite 'go-behind' or asking what's the best 'take down' you know. But perhaps her finest recommendation is her sense of humor which manifests itself rarely, but is sharp, dry, and always to the point."

Smith goes on to retell the story of how Mars broke into the business, how she was in Sarasota, Florida, when she met the greatest of all the lady wrestlers. Here's where the article becomes very interesting. This time, the story is not about the legendary Mildred Burke. It's about the newly crowned June Byers.

"June Byers was visiting the circus winter headquarters. We got together after she had seen my trapeze act, and [she] sold me on gal grappling."

Yes, the origin story Mars had told many times now read that June Byers was responsible for her career. And it gets even better. "Frankly, Smithy, I didn't think I had qualified for the game, even after my first six matches, but my good friend June Byers was keeping an eye on me."

Sound familiar yet?

"June worked out with me, taught me plenty, encouraged me all she could, had me ringside when she was wrestling. I well remember one of her matches. it began with her opponent slamming her around a couple of times, and I thought she was in for a tough time, but she was just waiting for her adversary to drop her guard... and when she did, the bout was over with June the winner in less than a minute. Since that day, I've patterned my wrestling after hers."

The question here isn't whether Mars changed her story or not. There's enough evidence the 1954 article was recycling material from the 1952 column to prove Smith had not conducted a new interview. The question then becomes, why was this interview with Mars recycled and revised?

Charles A. Smith was a London-born sports writer who moved to New York after the end of World War II. He spent time as a banker before going to work for fitness magazine publisher Joe Weider, writing and editing stories for *Your Physique, Muscle Power, Muscle Builder, Mr. America, The Weightlifter,* and *Boxing and Wrestling.* He was editor-in-chief for the Wrestling portion of *Boxing and Wrestling* when both articles ran in the magazine, a powerful and influential voice in the world of pro wrestling.

Is it any wonder Mildred Burke never stood a chance when Billy Wolfe decided to cut her out of the business?

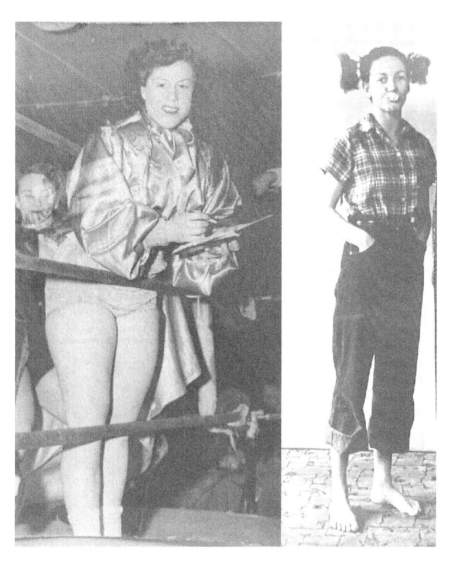

Left: Mars signing autographs. (Courtesy Marcella Foreit Robinette.)
Right: Bare footed, gum-smacking Daisy Mae.

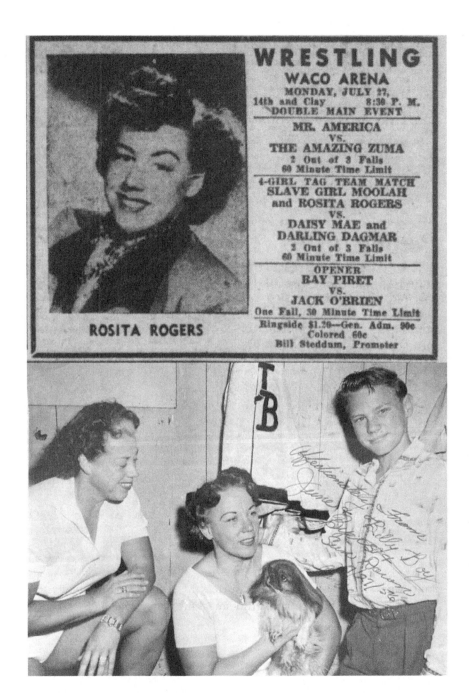

Top: Mars advertised as Rosita Rogers: Bottom: Mars with June Byers and her son Billy. (Courtesy Marcella Foreit Robinette.)

Mars got to the beach and soaked up the sun at every opportunity.
(Courtesy Marcella Foreit Robinette.)

Mars missed it up with wrestlers, refs, and promoters. (Courtesy Marcella Foreit Robinette.)

Mars and Mae Young. (Courtesy Marcella Foreit Robinette.)

"I've had lotsa chances, but I'd rather wait until the right guy comes along. So far I haven't met him, but I'm waiting."

Those are the words Mars Bennett spoke to Charlie A. Smith during their first interview for *Boxing and Wrestling* magazine back in 1952 when he asked if Mars had found her special someone. Like most wrestlers, Mars probably would not have admitted if she indeed had a special someone at that time. It's long been common practice for wrestlers to conceal their personal lives because the illusion of being single was good for business - at the box office, and after hours at the hotel.

Mars would never marry, but two men managed to put a ring on her finger for a short time. One of the two made his living placing rings on fingers. Not only placing, but designing said rings, so it's very likely he had something to do with Mars being referred to as the girl with the million dollar diamonds. He was a jeweler, and he greatly enjoyed making special items to share with his beloved Mars.

While involved with the jeweler, Mars also designed some of her own jewelry. One of the most spectacular pieces she created was a ring adorned with sapphires and diamonds. "It looked like fireworks," says Marcella Foreit Robinette. "It was so beautiful. When Mars died, Loa Vivian gave it to Mrs. Walkowe." Mars also had horseshoe rings made for herself and Loa Vivian. Those rings were passed down to Anton V's daughters, Loa and Marcella, when Loa Vivian died.

The jeweler made a gorgeous ring with three large diamonds surrounded by nine small diamonds. Mars's sister-in-law wears that ring today. "My mom can't wear it anywhere without someone making a comment about that ring," says Marcella Foreit Robinette.

Mars gave Belle Drummond an opal bracelet. Later in life it became an indispensable part of Belle's daily attire.

Mars was also engaged to a stand-up comic best known at the time for his celebrity impressions. Born in the Bronx on January 23, 1923, the young comedian attended school with future television star Don Adams, who became a lifelong friend. He also served his country in World War II on a submarine tender alongside another future star, fellow

New Yorker Bernard Schwartz. Schwartz shared the young comedian's dream of one day being a star, but the comedian considered his odds to be slim. Schwartz would become famous after taking the stage name Tony Curtis, and he would often help his former shipmate secure roles in his films.

The comedian didn't change his name much when he entered show business. Instead of Lawrence, he went by the nickname Larry, and he kept his last name: Storch. At the time he met Mars, Larry Storch was working the clubs doing comedy and celebrity impressions. It wasn't until after Mars died that he became a household name, making numerous guest appearances on TV before becoming immortal as Corporal Agarn on the hit TV series *F-Troop*.

In the early 1990s Storch went on tour in a production called *Breaking Legs*. When the show came to the Fisher Theater in Detroit, Marcella and some relatives went to see the play. The next day, Marcella called the theater and left a message for him. To her surprise, Larry called back. "He was so nice," she says. "He asked me what I was doing that night. I said nothing. He knew I had seen the show already, but he told me he would leave tickets for me at the box office. They were front row center seats!"

Larry asked Marcella to come backstage afterwards. "He was so nice. He told me I looked and talked a lot like Mars, which my dad had always said."

Arguably the biggest star Mars became acquainted with was a humble boy from West Tennessee who would soon become the biggest music star in the world: Elvis Presley. Belle Drummond was especially infatuated with the handsome young crooner. Elvis Presley was a wrestling fan himself, and he loved the lady wrestlers. He even dated Penny Banner for a time.

"Elvis wanted them to teach him how to wrestle, but they never got the chance because they were all so busy," says Mars Belle, recalling the stories her mom used to tell. "She also told me that when a car they owned got wrecked, Elvis offered to buy them a new one. Mars and Belle told him no!"

Belle loved to brag about her friendship with Elvis. "We met him in Knoxville and Chattanooga just after he made 'Teddy Bear,'" she told an interviewer in 1980. "I cried my eyes out when he died." Belle kept an autograph from Elvis in her scrapbook, along with her many news clippings and photos.

Belle and Mars had their share of romances, but the greatest love they found was with one another. The two became more than just best friends. They became partners.

Belle never spoke about her relationship with Mars to her daughter, and if Mars's family knew about it, her brother never said a word. There were plenty of clues. Mars and Belle owned a car together, with both their names on the title. They also bought a house together complete with a workout room that included weights and practice mats. They adopted a pair of Boston terriers named Buster and Booly who became their mascots. When the girls would practice wrestling, the dogs would often join them on the pats.

It wasn't until Mars Belle Drummond went to a gathering of the Ladies International Wrestling Association in Las Vegas that she knew anything of Mars and Belle's true connection. "I met Ella Waldek, and she made a comment insinuating that they were in a relationship. A few years later, I met a lady on Facebook who had been a psychiatric nurse for my mother. She's the one who told me Mars and Belle were actually partners."

Coming out publicly would never have been an option during that time; it would have been career suicide. But the girls made the best of things, sharing rides, rooms, and plenty of adventures on the road.

Mars and Belle were hardly the only same sex couple in pro wrestling at that time. Ruth Boatcallie and Carol Cook, who were close friends with Mars, were also a couple. They split up after many years together, but the break up was amicable. Ruth's niece, who has kept the story of her wrestling aunt alive, still refers to Cook as Aunt Carol.

By contrast, the relationship between Olga Zepeda and China Mira ended in cold-blooded murder. Mira shot Zepeda to death in the home they shared in New Orleans. Reports said the ladies got into a dispute over a dog, but hindsight says it was probably more than that.

Mars and Belle only had a few short years together, but by all accounts, they were happy times. "Mom told me some crazy stories," says Mars Belle. "They went into a bar one time where they were regulars. Some bikers started razzing them, giving them a hard time. The bartender knew Mars and my mom, and he kept telling the guys, 'I wouldn't mess with them if I were you.

"The guys wouldn't leave Mars and Mom alone. They kept messing with them, and finally, the girls snapped. They cleaned house! They were tossed in jail that night, and the Billy Wolfe had to bail them out because they had a match the next day. He wasn't very happy about it."

On another occasion, the girls went into a New York City bar barefoot. A couple of guys noticed the girls' feet and came over to chat with them.

"What do you girls do for a living?" one of the men asked.

"We sell shoes," said the girls.

Mars and Belle had some matching ring attire made for their tag team matches. One piece from that ensemble gave young Mars Belle nightmares. "Mars and Mom had these purple capes that had dragons on them with orange flames coming out of their mouths. Mom had hers hanging up in our house. They were very colorful, but they looked kind of evil. I was scared to death of them as a kid.

"At that time I didn't know anything about my mom's past as a professional wrestler, but from that cape, I knew she had done something interesting."

Both Mars and Belle were off the road for nearly a year and a half, dropping out of the scene in the summer of 1954 and returning together in February of 1956. It's unclear why they would have taken such a long leave of absence. There are whispers of medical issues, but there are no diaries or records to confirm. It's unlikely two such characters, who loved the road and enjoyed having adventures, were simply sitting at home. They may have gone west to try their luck in Hollywood. Or perhaps Mars took Belle with her back to the circus for a time.

"I used to live in Bradenton, Florida," says Mars Belle. "I went to the Ringling Museum down in Florida once, and I know damn well I saw a picture on the wall of my mom and Mars standing outside a tent."

A year and a half after her title match with June Byers, Mars Bennett returned to the ring. It was February of 1956, and Mars teamed up with Belle Drummond in Dayton, Ohio, to face a pair of sisters forging their own uncharted path.

For all his faults, Billy Wolfe did a few things that were worthy of praise. One of his most notable accomplishments was integrating the women's wrestling ranks in the 1950s. Billy Wolfe not only brought African American women into the business, he got them booked in the ring with his top stars.

Betty Wingo was the oldest of three sisters and the first to enter the wrestling game. Born in Georgia, the family moved to Columbus, Ohio where Betty, sisters Ethel and Marva, and their friend Kathleen Wimbley all began training at the local YMCA in judo, strength training, gymnastics, and wrestling.

The girls caught the eye of Billy Wolfe, and one by one the ladies turned pro. Betty changed her first name to become Babs Wingo. Sister Ethel changed her last name to hide her relationship with Babs, becoming Ethel Johnson. Marva, the youngest, became Marva Scott. Their stories were recently chronicled in a documentary by filmmaker Chris Bournea called *Lady Wrestler* that's worth seeing.

Babs Wingo and Ethel Johnson became the first two women to break the color barrier in women's wrestling, with both receiving title shots against Mildred Burke before she was dethroned. By 1956 they were becoming successful draws themselves. A show headlined by Babs and Ethel in Kansas City drew 9000 fans in 1954.

Babs and Marva were booked against Mars and Belle in Dayton on February 21, 1956, but due to an illness, Marva Scott substituted for Ethel. Babs and Marva defeated Mars and Belle, taking two out of three falls. In the main event, the real "Mr. America" Gene Stanlee fought another African American hero Bobo Brazil to a time limit draw.

Mars and Belle also worked a few singles matches across Ohio that month, including a bout in Painsville that was photographed for a new wrestling publication. Issue number one of *Girl Wrestlers* debuted on newsstands in 1954 at the low price of thirty-five cents and featuring

"137 sizzling, uncensored pics." The magazine cover also promised stories on popular stars like June Byers, Penny Banner, Belle Starr, Babs Wingo, Moolah. Lee Chona LeClaire, Bonnie Watson, and Ethel Brown.

Under the banner headline "Conquest of Mars," a six paragraph story sheds light on the curly-headed blonde Belle Drummond, still largely unknown to wrestling fans at the time.

"Belle is a descendant of the Second Family of Scotland, the Clan Drummond, a justly famed fighting family. Belle has inherited her aggressiveness, her physical stamina, and her intestinal fortitude from her Scottish ancestors.

"One of Belle's lifelong dreams is to go to Scotland and visit the Drummond Castle; to stay with Sir John Drummond, the head of her clan, and to learn the Scottish customs, the family dances and traditions."

It sounds like a lot of ballyhoo, like the kind of backstory Jack Pfefer or Vince McMahon would invent for the sake of selling a new star, but it's all true. Belle Drummond did trace her lineage back to Clan Drummond, and it had always been a dream to visit Drummond Castle and estate, first built in 1490 in Perthshire, Scotland that boasts one of the most beautiful formal gardens in all of Great Britain.

Girl Wrestlers doesn't skimp on the photos either. Sixteen photos spread over eight pages tell the tale of the ladies and their battle in Painesville, Ohio. Referee Gypsy Daccaro even gets in on the action, seen numerous times trying to get Mars to play by the rules while Mars sneers and whispers back, "I told ya to leave me alone." Elsewhere, Gypsy Daccaro is pictured giving Mars a boot to the head during a particularly contentious point in the bout.

The packed publication also features photo essays of June Byers, Betty Hawkins, Nell Stewart, and Moolah as well as three different battle royals, one of which is an all African-American affair with Babs Wingo, Ethel Johnson, Betty White, Louise Green and Kathleen Wimbley.

After a few more tag matches around Ohio, Mars and Belle headed south to Florida. They met up with Judy Glover, Dot Dotson, Libby Gonzales, China Mira, and Barbara Baker to work some tag matches as well as battle royals. A few of those shows, including the one held at the Eau Gallie Civic Center in Orlando, featured all seven women in "sportsdom's nearest approach to a female free-for-all."

The stakes were high for the seven-woman melee, as the first lady pinned in the battle royal would not only be done for the night but out of the money for the evening. The next two eliminated would meet in a singles clash, and the third and fourth women eliminated would team up against the last two standing in a tag match.

"It's speed on the large scale and a match that referees try to avoid," said *The Orlando Sentinel*. "The men in white trousers don't volunteer for this one - they have to be drafted."

After making the rounds in a series of battle royals, Mars and the girls split off into tag teams and singles contests across the Florida territory. In Tampa Mars defeated Judy Glover, a veteran of the U.S. Air Force, to earn a promised title shot against June Byers. Down in St. Lucie, she earned a title shot in a less conventional way. She defeated Barbara Baker twice, first in a singles match, and then in a mixed tag in which the ladies were paired up with midget wrestlers. Mars and Fuzzy Cupid came out the winners over Baker and Cowboy Bradley.

Sadly, the Florida fans were denied a chance to see Mars challenge June Byers for the title. The St. Lucie paper reported that Byers had suffered an injury in St. Paul, Minnesota, but in truth, Byers was out west where she had defended her title against Penny Banner in Albuquerque the night before the promised title bout. The substitute for Byers was Verne Bottoms, a relative newbie from Tennessee who had taken on an old pseudonym briefly used by Mars.

Mars and Belle left Florida in mid-April, taking their feud to Arkansas, Alabama, Tennessee, Missouri, and Kansas. "Two ladies meet on an hour long, best two-out-of-three match," *The Courier News* in Blytheville, Arkansas declared on April 16. "They're Miss Mars Bennett and Miss Belle Drummond. Chances are tonight both ladies will forget they're ladies or that they ever heard the word before."

The Courier News came back a few days later with more on Mars Bennett, who once again credited Jack Dempsey with getting her into the business. She told the paper she still kept in touch with Dempsey, who checked in on Mars to see how her career was going. When the paper asked if Mars had ever been seriously injured, she pointed to two lacerations on her face, one over each eye. Given she was feuding with Belle Drummond at the time, it's likely her best friend had something to do with those gashes.

In most cities Mars and Belle were either the main event or the semi-final, and they always stole the show. An ad in the Sedalia, Missouri newspaper proclaimed, "The weaker sex provides mat thrills galore," while *The Wichita Eagle* gushed in praise while promoting a second appearance by Mars.

"Fans were wowed by the fast moving antics of Miss Bennett in her debut match last Monday night. She turned cart wheels, pinwheels, and skipped through various didoes after flipping her foe to the mat. In fact, Miss Bennett is just about the fastest working competitor among the wrestlers on the distaff side to show in the Forum in quite some time. Her speed is amazing."

Mars locked up with Mary Jane Mull in Waco, Texas on May 14 in a contest to determine a challenger for June Byers and her World Championship. "This bout positively will not be televised," the ad declared in all caps. Mars got the victory, and this time, she also got her title shot against Byers.

Mars wrestled June Byers several times that month, locking up in Waco, Houston, Dallas, San Antonio, and Corpus Christi. The Women's World Championship was on the line every night, and not surprisingly, Byers came out the victor every time.

Mars and Belle moved on to Louisiana in late May and Mississippi in June, resuming their singles rivalry. It was Belle's first time in the state, and a heel Mars Bennett insured the fans were solidly behind the new girl. In Shreveport Mars won the first fall, but Belle took the second and third, surviving a series of head butts to the stomach in the final fall.

"What did ya expect?" Mars groused after the loss. "She's 25 pounds heavier than me!"

Having lost matches to Belle from Alexandria, Louisiana to Jackson, Mississippi, Mars headed back to home base in Ohio. Reconnecting with Penny Banner, Millie Stafford, and other members of Billy Wolfe's crew, she worked in a number of tag team matches, including a six-woman tag in Dayton.

Mars then traveled north of the border to Canada with Bonnie Watson, Penny Banner, and June Byers to work for Stu Hart, who had a surprise waiting for the girls when they arrived. Bonnie Watson and Penny Banner had been a big hit as a tag team in Alberta during their previous visit, so Hart had decided to promote the girls as the Women's Tag Team Champions. As Penny Banner wrote in her autobiography *Banner Days*, Hart told the girls, "This is my territory and my promotion, and I want to create the first Women's Tag Champions." Banner and Watson, who had matching outfits made for the trip, were thrilled.

Hart booked the ladies in Yellowknife, the capital and only city in Canada's Northwest Territories. The city is located on the north shore of Great Slave Lake about 250 miles from the Arctic Circle. It was named after the people of the Yellowknife Dene First Nation. The trip included a drive to Prince George followed by two flights, the last of which was on a sea plane. Mars and Penny Banner went first, sharing a flight to their final destination. The plane had no seats in the back, just two benches running along each side of the cabin. Mars tried to relax in the back while Penny sat next to the pilot.

The girls woke up the next morning to the sound of a marching band. They looked outside and were surprised to see a parade in progress. This was the first time the people of Yellowknife would see women's wrestling in person, and the ladies received a warm reception. Mars and Penny wrestled one on one that night, the first women to do so in that area. The next night, June Byers and Bonnie Watson joined them, with Banner and Watson defending their newly minted tag team title successfully.

Mars and the gang flew back to Calgary for the Stampede, one of the largest and most important cultural events in all of Canada. The ladies participated in the Stampede parade and wrestled over two nights. June Byers defended her title against Penny Banner on July 9. Mars teamed with June against Penny and Bonnie on July 10, with Penny and Bonnie successfully defending their Tag Team Championship against Mars and June.

The girls also worked in Edmonton and Vancouver, wrestling the same matches they had in Calgary. Penny Banner put up a game effort but just couldn't secure the win over June Byers. She had better luck with her partner as she and Bonnie Watson continued to defend their Tag Team Championship against June and Mars, Mars always taking the final pin, allowing the champion June Byers to remain protected.

In August the same four ladies headed south, where they changed up partners for another round of tag matches. In Arizona June Byers teamed up with Penny Banner, and Bonnie Watson joined forces with Mars. They switched back in Las Vegas and New Mexico, where June Byers and Mars Bennett were advertised as the Women's Tag Team Champions.

The Albuquerque Tribune sports editor sent a reporter named Beverly Wilkinson to cover the action when the girls hit town. Wilkinson had never attended a wrestling show before, but it's clear from her coverage she came away with a great appreciation for what she saw.

"Fine arts and wrestlers have two things in common: 1. They both work on canvas. 2. They both produce something worth watching.

The grunt, groan, and guttural growl artists spout sputum like Old Faithful spurts water. Spitting, nose blowing, sweating, straining - almost anything goes - on the mat at a wrestling match. But it's all part of the 'greatest show on earth.'"

Ms. Wilkinson went on to suggest she actually witnessed two "greatest shows on earth" at the Armory. There was the action on the canvas, which she clearly enjoyed, and the action in the crowd. "The audience gets in the act too. Cheers, jeers. Advice that's not too nice... 'Break it off, Danno.' 'Hit 'im in the gizzard.' 'Do the same thing to him.' 'Choke, choke.'"

Mars moved east from New Mexico to West Texas along with Bonnie Watson. Mars defeated Bonnie in the main event on August 20, 1956, in Abilene. Incredible as it sounds, the ladies went on right after Dory Funk, Sr., wrestled Bob Orton, Sr., reportedly for the very first time.

The ladies engaged in a singles feud and participated in a couple of mixed tag matches. In Lubbock Bonnie and Ray "Big Train" Clements took on Mars and Tommy Phelps. Sonny Myers teamed with Bonnie Watson in San Angelo, where Mars teamed up with Ricki Starr. Starr was also teamed up with Mars in Amarillo on August 23 where the duo faced Bonnie Watson and the legendary Dory Funk, Sr. Mars and Ricky were declared the winners when Funk threw a punch at Ricki Starr and struck Mars by mistake.

Talk about the girl with the iron jaw!

DEATH MATCH BENNETT

In September of 1956, Mars Bennett and Bonnie Watson traveled to Florida where they continued their feud in singles, tags, and battle royals. Olga Zepeda, Yoli Perez, and Sylvia Torres joined Mars and Bonnie for a five-woman tussle in Orlando and Fort Myers, where the first girl was done for the night and the next four paired off in singles matches based on their elimination.

Mars and Bonnie also teamed up for a few tag matches. In Tampa, Bonnie Watson had Sylvia Torre in a headlock when Mars accidentally drop-kicked her partner instead of Torre. Torre seized the moment and pinned Watson, scoring a victory for her and partner Ollie Perez. Watson then went after Mars, and the girls had to be pulled apart by referee Ike Eakin and promoter Pat O'Hara.

The following week, Bonnie and Mars met to settle their differences in what Pat O'Hara claimed was the first ever Women's Texas Death Match. The rules for the match stated there would be no time limit and pin falls could not end the match. The ladies would fight until one of them gave up or fell over from exhaustion. The equivalent to today would be a "Last Woman Standing" match where two ladies fight until one cannot answer a ten count.

The match at Gable Armory took place before a meager crowd of 600 fans. The girls wrestled through seven pin falls: four won by Watson and three by Mars. After the seventh fall, Watson threw Mars out of the ring. Injured, Mars was unable to crawl back in the ring, and Watson was declared the winner.

In Orlando the girls had another grudge match sparked by the outcome of a battle royal. Watson was the first lady eliminated as the other four girls, including Mars, jumped her at the outset. Watson accused Mars of turning the other girls against her and challenged Mars, who won the battle royal to a match. Mars agreed, promising to shut Bonnie's big mouth.

The day before the show, promoter Cowboy Luttrall told The Orlando Sentinel the ladies got into fisticuffs in his office. "The two clashed in his office 'like a couple of teased rattlesnakes.' [Luttrall] reported they pulled hair and struck each other."

Mars and Bonnie took their rivalry to Alabama and Kentucky in October. Bonnie won the majority of their singles battles, but Mars came out the victor in tag team matches that saw Mars team up with Penny Banner and Bonnie with Ella Waldek.

By mid-October of 1956, they went their separate ways, with Mars returning to Florida to feud with Therese Theis. Mars lost the match, and a chance to face June Byers again, in Tampa when she missed a drop kick and was pinned in the third and deciding fall, but Mars came out on top in the majority of their confrontations.

Mars wrestled Ella Waldek in another swing through Cowboy Luttrall's territory. Waldek fared better against Mars than Therese Theis thanks partly to Mars and her dirty tactics. In most matches Mars lost at least one fall via disqualification. In Orlando Mars lost the second fall against Waldek when she refused to let go of a choke hold. She came back in the third with another choke hold, and Waldek finally had enough. "I'll teach 'em to choke me!" she cried out after dropping Mars with an atomic drop to secure the final fall.

Mars capped off the month of October wrestling Therese Theis on live TV in Tampa, appearing on the weekly wrestling program broadcast on Channel 8. The girls were the featured attractions at all of these shows. Meanwhile, a blonde brute trained by Buddy Rogers was working on all of the undercards: future Hall of Famer Ray Stevens.

Mars and Ella teamed up in early November, meeting Therese Theis and Joyce Smith in a tag match in Tampa. The match ended without a winner as all four ladies crashed the ring in the third and final fall. Referee and wrestler Doc Dogienero found himself in the middle of the brawl and called for the bell, ending the action at one fall apiece. The melee got so heated Therese Theis had to be carried out of the ring by referee Dogienero.

Doc Dogienero was on hand in Orlando for another match between the four ladies, but on that night it was promoter Milo Steinborn who donned the referee's jersey. The ladies switched partners, with Mars and Therese taking on Ella and Joyce, but the result was the same. Things began to unravel when Therese choked Ella with the tag team rope, holding her tight while Mars pummeled Ella with her fists. Unable to get Mars and Therese to set Ella free, Steinborn called for the bell.

Ella Waldek finally broke free of the role and went after Mars, slamming her to the mat, stomping on her, and reigning blows down on her. Steinborn and Theis had to step in, with Theis pulling Mars to the locker room while Steinborn escorted Waldek to hers.

Steinborn wasted no time scheduling a rematch between Mars and Ella. It would be the second death match held in Orlando and the first to feature two ladies. The same rules applied as when Mars faced off with Bonnie Watson; the only way to win was to make sure your opponent couldn't continue.

The ladies wrestled for twenty-three minutes, and Mars scored three pin falls versus two for Ella. Alas, pin falls did not count in this confrontation, and the winner would be the first to incapacitate their opponent. Waldek went to work on Mars's left leg, kicking her repeatedly in the left leg until her left thigh hemorrhaged. Mars was unable to continue, and Waldek was declared the winner.

Mars was absent from the Florida wrestling scene for the next two weeks, either selling a false injury or nursing a real one. At the end of November she clashed with Penny Banner in Biloxi, Mississippi, where she dropped a singles match to Banner in two straight falls. Banner scored the first fall via pin and was awarded the second after Mars drop-kicked referee Pat Newman in the back.

In December 1956 Mars teamed up with a few former rivals in tag matches across Florida, teaming up with Bonnie Watson, Therese Theis, and Penny Banner. Banner and Bennett met up with Olga Zepeda and Therese Theis in Fort Myers on December 4 in another slug fest that ended with no decision. Tied at two falls a piece, the match broke down with Banner and Zepeda fighting in the ring while Mars and Therese brawled on the outside.

"The wild affair between Bennett and Theis outside the ring was by far the hottest action of the night as several good stiff punches were landed before police and promoter Pat O'Hara, plus a few fans, separated the two," proclaimed the Fort Myers *News-Press*.

Pat O'Hara decided there was only one way to resolve the matter between Mars and Therese Theis: a Texas Death Match! "Fight to the finish. Falls don't count," read the newspaper ads. "No time limit to win. One's opponent must give up or drop from exhaustion. New referee." Ticket prices ranged from $2 for reserved seating down to fifty cents for kids.

Mars scored the first two falls in the December 11 bout, with Theis winning the third. During the fourth fall, Mars missed a tackle and flew outside the ring. The injured Mars was unable to continue, and Theis was declared the winner.

Mars ended 1956 with a bang, competing in another battle royal for Pat O'Hara in Fort Myers on Christmas night. China Mira, Ella Waldek, Therese Theis, and Judy Glover joined her for the melee as the girls spent the holiday away from home. The Fort Myers paper didn't carry the results, but as per usual, the first girl out was done for the night, with the remaining four pairing up in singles matches based on where they were eliminated.

Two things are certain. One, the ladies put on a hell of a show for the holiday crowd. And two, Angelo Martinelli and Frenchy Roy had no chance of upstaging the girls as the only other match on the card.

Mars and Belle Drummond in the dragon capes that used to terrify
Belle's daughter Mars Belle.

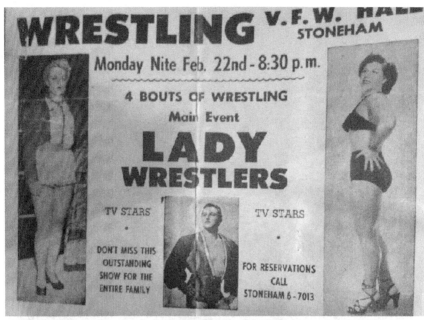

Top: Belle Drummond and Mars advertised together. Bottom: Mars and Larry Storch are on the left, with Belle on the right. (Courtesy Mars Belle Drummond.)

Belle Drummond's address book included both Jack Pfefer and Elvis Presley. (Courtesy Mars Belle Drummond.)

Belle takes Mars down hard in the pages of *Girl Wrestler*, 1954.

Top: Dot Dotson, Olga Zepeda, China Mira, Belle Drummond's sister Peggy, Mars, and Belle. (Courtesy Marcella Foreit Robinette.) Bottom: Mars (center) clowning around with one of the "mascots" she owned with Belle. (Courtesy Mars Belle Drummond.)

Top: Mars poses with the station wagon she owned with Belle
Drummond. Bottom: Mother Loa Vivian and Mars at the beach.
(Courtesy Marcella Foreit Robinette.)

Promotional photo. (Courtesy Marcella Foreit Robinette.)

Relaxing at home. (Courtesy Marcella Foreit Robinette.)

Mars remained in the Southeastern US at the start of 1957. She battled China Mira and Joyce Glover in singles competitions across the Sunshine State while wrestling Ella Waldek in Alabama and Tennessee. New girls like Kitty Powell, Joyce Braggs, Elaine Ellis, and Patty Neff took their lumps working with Mars, Judy Glover, Dot Dotson, and Therese Theis in tag matches and five- and six-woman battle royals.

Mars made another televised appearance in Tampa on January 26, when she teamed up with Patty Neff to wrestle Judy Glover and Elaine Ellis. Mars and Patty lost in two out of three falls in the main event broadcast on WFLA Channel 8. Wilbur Snyder also appeared on the show, wrestling Ike Eakins to a draw.

Snyder's future business partner appeared on a show in Orlando with Mars a week later. Dick the Bruiser, a former Green Bay Packer, wrestled Roy McClarity, a former Canadian hockey player. McClarity's wife Shirley Strimple wrestled Mars on the same card.

The two ladies wrestled to a draw on Monday night, February 4 in Tampa. This star-studded card included a clash between Dick the Bruiser and Wilbur Snyder as well as a title match between World Champion Lou Thesz and Buddy Rogers.

The ladies were no longer working as many main events as they once had, but they were still stealing the show, even in the opening matches. Mars drew rave reviews for her bouts with Judy Glover, and the battle royals continued to be crowd pleasers.

Mae Weston joined the ladies in late February, working in tags and battle royals with Mars and the other ladies. One of the long-time members of Billy Wolfe's crew, Mae had one of the longest careers of any lady wrestler, starting in the 1930s as a challenger to Clara Mortensen and ending up as Ma Bass, matriarch of wrestling's notorious Bass family in the 1970s. Ma Bass even laced up the boots a few times in six-person tag matches with her adopted wrestling sons Ron and Donnie.

Mars had her own feud with Mae Weston in March of 1957. A crowd of 1237 turned out in Orlando to see Mae defeat Mars. That same night, Mars got to visit with another old friend backstage. Jack Dempsey worked on the show as the special guest referee in the main event where Fred Atkins defeated Frank Taylor.

In March Mars left Florida to team up with June Byers in Tennessee. The Women's Champion tagged up with Mars in Nashville against Bonnie Watson and Millie Stafford before defending her title against Mars in Chattanooga.

The move to Tennessee from Florida marked another turning point for Mars. The landscape of women's wrestling was changing quickly at that time. As Billy Wolfe's influence decreased, his grip on the women's wrestling business slipped away. Mars was no longer working through Billy Wolfe. She was working directly for Nashville wrestling office.

The Nashville territory was run by Nick Gulas and Roy Welch. The partners kept an office just off the lobby of the Maxwell House Hotel where Christine Jarrett handled ticket sales for the weekly shows. Gulas and Welch booked the ladies direct instead of going through Billy Wolfe.

Belle Starr jumped ship from Wolfe to Gulas around the same time, and in 2007, she told Jamie Hemmings of Slam! Wrestling why she (and most likely Mars) made the move.

"I stayed [with Billy Wolfe] only a year. Then I went to work for what they called Opposition, Nick Gulas, out of the Nashville territory. The reason for that is Billy Wolfe took forty percent of our money. It was a booking fee that he charged. It was not fair that he took that much money. I resented the fact that I had to give him that because we worked so hard for our money."

Not surprisingly, Belle Drummond made the jump to Gulas and Welch as well. She met up with Mars on the road in Huntsville, Alabama, and the ladies joined up with Dot Dotson, China Mira, and Sylvia Torres for a five-woman battle royal. Belle had a short night as the first girl eliminated, while Mars went on to face China Mira in a singles match as the last two survivors. Mira pinned Mars in ten minutes of action.

In May of 1957, Mars wrestled Lady Angel, one of Jack Pfefer's most infamous creations. Hailed as the ugliest woman alive, Lady Angel was a bald woman out of the same character mold as The French Angel Maurice Tillet and other wrestling angels. She was billed at six feet in height and towered over the majority of her competition. "The only girl bald-headed coming from Europe - the horror face - she makes women feint, children cry, oh Mother look - a Lady Angel!"

Jack Pfefer was in Nashville at the time, staying at the same hotel where Gulas and Welch kept their offices, but according to Belle Starr, who never even crossed paths with Jack that summer, he wasn't working with Gulas and Welch. It's unclear why Pfefer was at the Maxwell House at that time. A decade later, he had a famous run-in with Christine Jarrett in the women's locker room when he tried unsuccessfully to extort money from her bosses.

Pfefer kept a few notes from Mars in his file from 1957, including a postcard Mars sent to him from the Virginia Court motel in Meridian, Mississippi.

Hi Jack -

Belle and I stayed here. It's a beautiful place with a new swimming pool. Got some sun. I've told Bibber McCoy about our packed houses in Nashville territory. I've got them "all shook up." Will write a letter and give you all the news.

Love, Mars

Pfefer also kept a letter she sent him from Atlanta, written on letterhead paper from Town & Country Hotel Courts. It appears that Pfefer had booked Mars down to Georgia for a few shows for good money. It appears from the contents of the letter Pfefer may have over-sold the opportunity.

May 28, 1957

Dear Bundles Sugar - Daddy - Jack -

Just a few lines to let you know everything is fine. Only no Bundles. This territory is really really bad. Here are my bookings. Mon, Augusta. (Tues off.) Wed - Valdosta. Thurs - Columbus. Fri - Marietta & Sat - Hogansville. See I told you I would not get Atlanta or Macon. They closed Atlanta down for a few weeks.

Will be back in Nashville Sunday morn. and will check with you then. Best to you and Ziggy.

Best regards,
Mars

Ziggy was a nickname for Stanislaus Zbyszko, a former wrestler who worked with Pfefer and had a hand in breaking Lady Angel into the business.

Mars worked with Barbara Baker on that her swing through Georgia, and the two were even in the main event in Hogansville. Even so, it was a bad week, and Mars was not happy about the lack of "bundles."

Mars did a lot of traveling in June. She was all over Florida, Alabama, Mississippi, Tennessee, and South Carolina. She worked Lady Angel in a number of towns where the Angel was making her debut, putting Pfefer's "grotesque" special attraction over. She also worked tags and singles, sharing the ring with old friends like China Mira, Millie Stafford, and Belle Drummond as well as newer ladies like Kathy Branch.

In July Mars joined up with the gum-smacking hillbilly Daisy Mae to tag team against Lady Angel. The Angel had a few different partners. One was Mars's old pal Millie Stafford. The other was twenty-one year old Belle Starr.

Belle Starr was a native of Ohio. Her mother was a professional bowler, and her father and brothers were all athletes. Starr played a lot of sports growing up herself, but the moment she saw professional wrestling, she knew she'd found her destiny. "I think the first wrestling match I saw might have been on television. I'm talking about the early '50s. I saw Mildred Burke and Mae Weston. Once I saw Nell Stewart, I said that's exactly what I want to do. She was so pretty and beautiful, I just wanted to be like her."

Starr attended a Catholic High School. She kept her dream a secret from her family, but she found encouragement from one of the nuns at school who encouraged her to follow her dream. Still under age, Belle signed up to train. Her mother noticed the bruises on their daughter's body after only a few weeks, and she was forced to tell her father. To her surprise, her dad did not immediately object. He told her if she kept her grades up, she could continue training. Belle studied harder than ever so she could pursue her dream.

Belle Starr's mom got credit for coming up with her ring name, and it was only later that she learned that Belle Starr had also been the name of a famous Western outlaw. She had green eyes and short, dark hair with an athletic physique. She was no stranger to Mars Bennett, having worked with her numerous times, and the two ladies became travel companions during that fateful summer.

"Mars was very nice. I liked her a lot. But she was tough in the ring," says Belle Starr about Mars. "She did a lot or aerial moves and flips. She was great to work with."

Mars continued to work mixed tag matches as well. She teamed up with Joe Costello to wrestle Cathy Branch and Tarzan Hewitt in Decatur, Alabama. She wrestled Daisy Mae and Farmer Jones twice, partnering with Black Bat in Chattanooga and Rowdy Red Roberts in Huntsville, Alabama. Mars also locked up with Dot Dotson and Verne Bottoms in addition to Belle Starr.

No matter what town, no matter who else was on the card, no matter what match she was in, Mars remained an attraction. If she wasn't in the main, she was in the featured spot. She turned 35 on August 3, but she was forever billed at the age of 27. Mars was evergreen in the eyes of promoters and fans.

From the Gulas/Welch home base in Nashville she traveled to Knoxville on August 16 with Belle Starr, where the ladies lost a tag match to Daisy Mae and Judy Glover. On August 22 she traveled to Bristol, Tennessee to wrestle a singles match against China Mira. The ladies drove through the night back to home base in Nashville to catch some sleep before heading out for their next booking.

It was the last trip home Mars would ever make.

THE ACCIDENT

Jack Pfefer had one more note from Mars in his personal files, a note she wrote to him after returning from Bristol early one morning. It was written on the Maxwell House hotel stationary:

7:45 AM

Jack-

Went back out to the tour motel.
Call me about 2:00 pm as I just got in from Bristol, Tenn.

Love,
Mars

P.S. Tell Nina where I'll be.

There's no date on the note, but even for a meticulous record keeper like Jack Pfefer, it's an odd one to retain on file. Mars had visited Bristol on a few occasions that summer. She could have left the note for him after any one of those occasions. That said, it's entirely possible Pfefer kept the note for a very sentimental reason: it may have been the last correspondence he ever received from her.

On the afternoon of August 23, 1957, Mars set out from Nashville behind the wheel of the station wagon she owned with Belle Drummond. Belle Starr was riding shot gun, and Larry Clark was in the back. Clark was new to the business, having left college to pursue his wrestling dream. Belle Starr remembers him as being handsome and very athletic.

The three were headed east on Highway 70 South to Greenfield, Tennessee, where Belle and Mars were scheduled to wrestle a tag match. Ten miles outside of Nashville, just at the foot of Nine Mile Hill, they were struck by a cement truck driving on the wrong side of the road. The truck hit the car head on.

The accident looked so bad, the passersby who stopped to help did not expect to find any survivors. "I was thrown through the windshield," says Belle Starr, who was found lying on the ground near the car. She was badly injured, but alive.

Larry Clark was in the backseat, and when help arrived at the car, he said he could not move his legs. He needed assistance to get out of the vehicle. He was moved to an ambulance and taken to the hospital.

According to Mars's family, Clark was seated directly behind Mars. When the truck hit the car head on, Clark hit the back of the driver's seat and broke it. Mars was crushed between the seat and the steering wheel. She never had a chance. After helping Clark out of the backseat, her body was removed from the vehicle.

Larry Clark and Belle Starr spent several weeks in the hospital. "I didn't know Mars was dead until the day after the accident," she says. "Larry couldn't move his legs, and they thought he might be paralyzed. He was on a board, and they had to turn him every day."

The newspapers reported that Mars had veered to the wrong side of the road when the collision occurred, but Frank Clark and Belle Starr both said Mars was not at fault. Mars's family refused to believe she was responsible as well. Her brother Anton V. made the trek down to Nashville to see the scene for himself. He examined the skid marks on the road, and he knew it was the truck driver's fault.

"He was driving drunk," says Marcella.

Two months later, three lawsuits were filed in a federal district court in Nashville. One suit came from Mars's mother, Loa V. Skiles. The other two were filed by Belle Starr and Larry Clark under their real names Patricia Penry and John H. Wilder. The three filed suit against the trucking company, Time, Inc, and the driver, Ernest Landis, Jr., seeking damages totaling half a million dollars.

Clark and Starr both testified that the truck driver had crossed the line and was at fault, but thanks to some shadiness between the trucking company and the judge, blame for the accident stuck to Mars.

Larry Clarke never wrestled again following the accident. Doctors feared he would never walk again, but Clark persevered and managed to get back up on crutches. He left the business of wrestling behind and went back to college to finish his degree.

After her discharge from the hospital, Belle Starr moved in with Nick Gulas and his wife, who generously opened their home to her. Starr remembers them very fondly. Her recovery was not brief, but in January of 1959 she returned to the ring and resumed her career.

Belle married fellow wrestler Juan Sebastian. When her daughter was born in 1966, she stepped away from the ring, but after her daughter turned seven, she went back out on the road. Belle Starr wrestled many more years, but never for Moolah, who took a percentage of the girls' money the same way Billy Wolfe had. In 2007 she was honored with the Pioneer Award from the Gulf Coast Wrestling reunion held in Mobile, Alabama.

Mars Bennett dreamed of the day she would retire to New York City. She planned to use the money she was saving from her wrestling career to open a high-end restaurant in the city. Mars was cremated, and her ashes were scattered in the Gulf of Mexico off the coast of Florida.

WHAT A LEGACY

Car accidents have always been an occupational hazard in the wrestling business. Many wrestlers have walked away from wrecks no one should have survived. Mars was not the first to die on the highway, and she certainly wasn't the last.

The death of her best friend and partner devastated Belle Drummond. For a time, she tried to carry on with her career. She wrestled in Florida in September and then went back to Nashville in October, wrestling a few matches with Penny Banner at the Ellis Auditorium. Alas, the loss of Mars took the joy out of wrestling for Belle. In the fall of 1957, she took off her boots for the last time.

"Mom said the best years of her life were those years she wrestled," says Mars Belle Drummond. "She got to wrestle in Canada, Cuba, and all over the U.S. But it just wasn't the same without Mars."

Belle Drummond's passion for grappling may have vanished, but her wanderlust did not. She remained on the move, becoming everything from a lumberjack in Maine to a carpenter to a truck driver, fulfilling the desire of her restless spirit to be always on the move.

"Mom lived with another woman named Grace Newman after Mars," says Mars Belle. "She was also married three times, the first and third time to the same man. I was born April 6, 1965. Grace had her first daughter Kim almost a year to the day later on April 5, 1966."

Belle was in California when she gave birth to her only child. "My mom was going to name me either April, Bethany, or Mars," says Mars Belle Drummond. "She went with Mars Belle. Lucky me. I hated my name growing up. I got teased so bad in school. The kids called me Uranus and Jupiter. My mom always said, 'You'll appreciate it one day,'but I always threatened to change it as soon as I turned eighteen."

Mars Belle sees things very differently now. "I love my name! There's not a day goes by that someone doesn't ask, 'Is that your real name?' And I get to tell their story. I am Mars and Belle's legacy, and as long as I am alive, they are too."

Belle Drummond kept a lot of photos, programs, and clippings from her career. She was very proud of the scrapbook that contains a lot of memories of herself and Mars. Her daughter treasures all of her mom's keepsakes and has photos of her mom and Mars hanging in the entry way of her home. "As you enter the foyer, I have Mars on one side, and Mom on the other side. I love to brag about my mom and tell people she was a professional wrestler. And I tell people about the woman she named me for."

Belle raised her daughter with the help of her own mom, who lived with her. Mars Belle never knew her father.

Belle Drummond always wanted to write her own book but never did. She developed schizophrenia in her later years, possibly due in part to her childhood traumas and head injuries suffered in the ring. Belle would sometimes have breakdowns and become violent, and her actions left her daughter with PTSD.

One night when her daughter was about seven, Belle woke everyone in the house around 3 a.m., throwing pots and pans in the kitchen. Mars Belle and her grandma found Belle having a breakdown in the kitchen, not wearing any clothes. Belle's mother called the police, warning them, "You're going to need to bring a lot of help. My daughter is a former professional wrestler."

The police didn't listen. "They sent Barney Fife," says Mars Belle. "He got too close, and Mom threw him clear across the room. It was a battle royal. She was right back in her wrestling days, and it took eight of them to finally get my mom under control."

On another occasion, Belle woke her daughter in the middle of the night shouting, "Mars! Mars! Help me! Help me! I'm having my baby!"

Mars Belle came running into her mom's bathroom, thinking her mother had fallen. She found Belle urinating on the toilet, screaming, "My water broke. I'm having my baby!"

"Mom," said Mars Belle, "You had a hysterectomy after you had me. You can't have another kid!"

"No, no, I'm serious!" said Belle. "I'm having my baby!"

Belle's mother came into the room. "What the hell's going on?"

Mars Belle said, "Mom's having a baby."

"Oh geez," said Belle's mother.

Mars Belle turned back to her mom. "Who's the father?"

Bell cried out, "Elvis Presley!"

In spite of the hardships, Mars Belle says that on her good days, her mom was the best mom ever. "She was very talented. She could play guitar and piano. Never had a lesson in her life, but she could play by ear." Belle also made sure her daughter was in church every week. "She couldn't go because of her mental health issues, but she always made sure I went."

Mars Belle suffered a lot of bullying in school. She'd come home hurt with her clothes torn, and Belle would ask why she didn't fight back.

"Mom," said Mars Belle, "The Bible says to turn the other cheek."

"Yeah, and if you don't do something, I'm gonna turn your other cheek red!"

Belle tried to teach her daughter a few wrestling moves for self-defense purposes, but Mars Belle resisted. "I wasn't as athletically gifted as her mother. I always told her I'd rather let someone beat me up than fight. That used to make my mom so mad."

Belle made sure the boys who dated her daughter knew that if anything happened to Mars Belle, they would answer to her. She'd literally grab them by the collar and tell them, "If you hurt my daughter, I'll break your neck!"

Nervous, the boys would reply, "Okay, Ms. Drummond, I'll have her home early!"

Belle Drummond died in 1984 at the age of 56. In an interview given four years before her death, Belle commented, "If I die tomorrow, I've lived, honey." She certainly lived a lot in her brief years on Earth.

A decade after Belle passed away, Mars Belle attempted to fulfill another of Belle's dreams, to reconnect with some of the wrestlers she had once known. Mars Belle began surfing the World Wide Web and made contact with The Fabulous Moolah herself. After talking with Moolah and Mae Young by phone, Mars Belle decided to attend the 1995 gathering of the Ladies International Wrestling Association in Las Vegas.

"I took a lot of mom's memorabilia with me to Vegas," says Mars Belle. "I had things with Moolah in them that she didn't have. Moolah wanted me to give it to her, and I had to say no. I couldn't give them up because it also had my mom and Mars."

Moolah convinced Mars Belle to come back the following year, saying that if she did, they would put Belle Drummond in the LIWA Women's Hall of Fame she was planning to establish in Columbia, South Carolina. Mars Belle was eager to do so, and on June 22, 1996, she received a plaque in honor of her mother at the LIWA banquet.

Mars Belle met many old friends of Mars and her mom in Vegas, including Moolah, Mae, Ella Waldek, Mae Weston, and Theresa Theis. She also swapped stories with pro wrestling historian and magazine editor Jim Melby and made friends with a young student of Moolah's named Joanie Laurer, who was just a few years away from becoming the ninth wonder of the world Chyna in WWF.

Mars Belle never met her namesake, but she got to know Mars's mother Loa, who lived in Florida. Belle and Loa remained in contact for years and exchanged letters. Mars Belle found some of the letters after her mom passed, including on where Loa describes finally receiving "my baby's ashes."

Loa never got over the death of her daughter. She was not ashamed of Mars in any way. The two had been very close, and the memory of her lost child was just too painful. Loa died in April of 1979 at the age of 79. She was cremated, and her ashes, along with those of Roy Skiles, were also scattered in the Gulf of Mexico off the Florida Coast, the same as Mars.

Despite her early death, the memory of Mars Bennett survived much longer than many of her contemporaries. She was one of the few women long-gone from this world to not only be mentioned but receive praise from her former rivals in the documentary *Lipstick and Dynamite*. Ida Mae Martinez, who has since passed, mentions Mars not only as a former circus performer and a tremendous athlete but as the woman who gave Ida Mae her first match.

Belle Starr never forgot Mars either. "She was a good wrestler," she told Slam! Wrestling's Jamie Hemmings. "Very athletic. Very tough." Gene Kiniski also spoke highly of Mars in later years, telling Slam's Greg Oliver she was "one tough son of a bitch."

Mars also gets a mention in *The Complete Idiot's Guide to Pro Wrestling* in a section that discusses the history of women's wrestling. Mars is mentioned along Mildred Burke, June Byers, Lilly Bitter, Dot Dotson (who they misspell as Cot Cotton), and another lady who passed away far too young, Elvira Snodgrass.

Some of the photos from the August 1948 issue of *Beauty Parade* were reprinted in *1000 Pin Up Girls*, a 2002 publication by Harald Hellman highlighting photo shoots from that bygone era. Readers of *The Wrestler, Inside Wrestling, Pro Wrestling Illustrated*, and other popular magazines of the 1980s may well have spotted Mars in the classifieds section where fans could buy or sell old issues of Boxing and Wrestling and other publications.

Mars made a number of television appearances in her career. So far, none of that footage has turned up on YouTube, but there are video tapes with footage of Mars in action in circulation. Marcella was able to get a copy of one of those videos.

"My father never saw Mars wrestle in person," says Marcella. "It was illegal for women to wrestle in many states, and he just never had the opportunity. I was able to order a video that had a match featuring Mars, and we got the whole family together to watch it. I remember my Dad kept going, 'Wow! Wow!' He always knew she was good because she was so athletic."

Anton V. was married three times. He had three children with his third wife: Anton, Loa, and Marcella, whose name was a tribute to Mars. He would have bought a farm and given his kids the same upbringing he had enjoyed on the farm with the Walkowe family if money allowed. Instead, he worked hard in the city of Detroit to provide for his wife and kids.

Anton V. was a devoted family man. When he and his co-workers got their checks on Friday, he ignored their jibes about being "whipped" and went home instead of out to the bar with the boys. "He would sit down and drink one beer at the table," says Marcella. "He'd pour a tiny bit in a shot glass for me, and I'd sip my beer while he drank his. Then he'd go outside and work in his garden."

Marcella and her siblings knew they had an aunt who died young, but they rarely heard any stories as children. Their father Anton V. was as tight lipped as his mother. He just never talked about it because it hurt too much.

One day, when Marcella was around eleven, her father gave her a box. "It seems like you should have this," he said. Marcella looked inside and was astonished at what she saw. It was filled with photos and memorabilia from her Aunt Mars and her careers in the circus and wrestling. Marcella couldn't help but notice just how much her aunt looked like her!

"My dad was not a religious man," said Marcella. "He believed in science. He believed in things he could see and touch. So it came as a shock when he told me why he'd given me all of Mars's things. He spotted me walking home from school one day and did a triple take. He thought I was his sister reincarnated. He said I talked like her, and I laughed like her. He said I was his sister made over. From then on, I started asking questions about Mars, and he would answer them."

Marcella had more than her looks and her manners in common with Mars. She always wanted to go fly fishing and enjoyed playing ice hockey. "My dad tried to discourage me from those things," she remembers. "He said they weren't lady like. I was a bit of a tomboy, but I was also a girly-girl. When I went fly fishing, I wore pink waders. When I played hockey, I wore red lipstick and bubblegum pink gloves. Those gloves made me a target, and the tougher girls would come out and try to hit me. I didn't care. I was like, 'Bring it on!'"

It was during the writing of this book Marcella and the Foreit family learned about Mars's relationship with Belle. Anton V. had always said Belle and Mars were best friends, but learning about their romantic relationship brought some powerful memories to mind for Marcella.

"When I was in college, I dated a guy who was mixed race. My parents disowned me for a while and tried to get me to break up with him. I didn't care. I was like Mars because I didn't take no for an answer. When I wanted something, I went out and got it.

"The relationship ended and I moved on. Years later, after I was married and had my four kids, my dad pulled me aside. 'I can't speak for your mother on this, but I want you to know the truth before I die,' he said. 'If you had married Joe, I would have loved him and your children, my grandchildren, just as much as I love my son-in-law and grandchildren. It wouldn't have mattered.'

"He then went on to say, 'Life is hard enough without other complications. You would have had trouble being accepted by society. I thought you were making a mistake, and I wanted to stop you from making a mistake. I am sorry if I was wrong.'"

Marcella thought of that story when she heard about Mars and Belle during the writing of this book. Says Marcella, "If she was gay, and if he knew, I am not sure he'd tell us. But I wonder if he saw Mars and Belle go through some of the struggles he tried to save me from. I know he saw a lot of Mars in me, and I wonder if he was trying to save me from some of the heartache and struggle she had."

Anton V. passed away on October 5, 2020 at the age of 99. Seven months prior to his passing, the world shut down due to the Covid-19 pandemic. Families were advised to quarantine and especially to stay away from elderly relatives due to the severity of the disease. The Foreit family chose to spend as much time with Anton V. as possible, deeming every day they had with him a gift not to be wasted. He passed away before Covid-19 started to ebb, but he never suffered from the dreaded virus.

Only a handful of people remain in the Foreit family who knew Mars in person, but her memory remains alive and well. This tight knit Midwestern family loves spending time together. They love swapping stories about family history, and the tales of Aunt Mars are always a hit. Not every family tree includes someone who joined the circus or became a professional wrestler. Mars did both, and the Foreit are proud of her legacy.

In an era when women were expected to fit a certain mold, Mars thumbed her nose at tradition. When her fellow riveters headed home to bake and clean house, Mars headed to the big top to ride elephants and soar on the flying trapeze. She took up fighting sports and became a pin up queen. And then, to top it all off, she became one of the top lady wrestlers of her day.

Mars left it all on the mat. She went where she wanted to go. She did what she wanted to do. She loved who she wanted to love. She was hardly done living when her life was taken from her on that Tennessee highway. If she could see the wrestling scene of today, where ladies not only work the main events but share the ring with men, she'd be very proud of the legacy she helped to forge.

She'd also be raring to go, ready to jump in that ring, take a few punches, and dish out a few of her own!

Mars Bennett - Girl Wrestler

Acknowledgements

This book would not have been possible had it not been for Elvira Snodgrass. It was during the writing of her biography that I found the photo of Mars Bennett published in the May 1949 edition of Picture Show that first caught my eye. Mars demanded my attention just as Elvira and The Black Panther Jim Mitchell had done when I wrote my first book Bluegrass Brawlers.

A huge, huge thank you to Chris Bergstrom, founder and manager of the Facebook Group Fabulous Ladies of Wrestling. Chris put me in touch with both Mars and Bell Drummond's survivors, who in turn provided not only a number of stories but the majority of photos in this book.

Thank you to Marcella Robinette for sharing your photos, your family tree research, and your family's memories of Mars.

Thank you to Mars Belle Drummond for sharing not only stories and photos of Mars but her own mother, the remarkable Belle Drummond.

Thank you to Greg Oliver for opening his files and sharing a wealth of yet-untold stories and quotes about Mars and Belle Starr. Thank you to Jamie Hemmings, who contributed to that research as well.

Thank you to Belle Starr, who shared her memories of Mars Bennett, the crash, Nick Gulas, and Elvira Snodgrass, who apparently gave her quite a beating!

Thank you to Jeff Leen, whose remarkable biography of Mildred Burke *The Queen of the Ring* proved to be an invaluable source on this book. I highly recommend it to anyone who wants more insight into the women's wrestling scene of the golden age as well as the life of the greatest of all lady wrestlers.

Penny Banner's book *Banner Days* also provided a few stories and additional clues about the life of Mars Bennett. It's a great read, if you can find it!

Thank you Princess Victoria, Vicki Otis, for writing the foreword. I would have loved to see you lock up with Mars!

Thank you to James Duncan for creating another outstanding book cover.

Additional thanks to Loa Foreit, Jimmy Wheeler, Kevin LaRose, Michael Norris, Lydia Cosper, Kim Goodwin Martin, Tamaya Greenlee, Mark James, Scott Teal, Ian Jedlica, the University of Notre Dame Library, the Circus Historical Society Facebook Group, and the Circus World Museum in Baraboo, Wisconsin.

About the Author

John Cosper is a wrestling blogger and historian whose other works include *Bluegrass Brawlers, Louisville's Greatest Show: The Story of the Allen Athletic Club, Grappling by Gaslight, Lord Carlton: Aristocrat of the Mat, The Ballad of Cousin Elvira,* and *The Original Black Panther*. He co-authored the biographies of Chris Candido (with Jonny Candido) and Wahoo McDaniel (with Karen McDaniel) as well as the autobiographies of Kenny "Starmaker" Bolin, "Dr. D" David Schultz, Tracy Smothers, Hurricane JJ Maguire, Mad Man Pondo, Scott Romer, and Princess Victoria. The best match he ever saw live was a falls count anywhere/ no disqualification match at Girl Fight Wrestling in Fort Wayne, Indiana, featuring Mickie Knuckles, Dementia D'Rose, Amazing Maria, and Samantha Heights. He lives in Southern Indiana, not far from Louisville, with his wife and two kids.

Visit his website at eatsleepwrestle.com

Made in the USA
Monee, IL
18 May 2025

17698505R00079